The Diary *of the*
Revd William Poole

The Diary *of the*
Revd William Poole

Perpetual curate *of the* parish
of HENTLAND & HOARWITHY

Introduced & edited by
REVD DR FRANCES PHILLIPS

LOGASTON PRESS

With thanks to FIONA, LADY MYNORS *for proofreading,*
and to TRACY SOMERVILLE *for the illustrations.*

First published 2024 by Logaston Press
The Holme, Church Road, Eardisley HR3 6NJ
www.logastonpress.co.uk
An imprint of Fircone Books Ltd.

ISBN 978-1-910839-79-9

Introduction text copyright © The Revd Dr Frances Phillips, 2024.

Designed & typeset by Richard Wheeler in 11.5 on 15 Jenson.
Cover design by Richard Wheeler.

Printed & bound in the UK.

Logaston Press is committed to a sustainable future for our business, our readers
and our planet. The book in your hands is made from paper certified by the
Forest Stewardship Council.

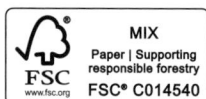

MIX
Paper | Supporting
responsible forestry
FSC
www.fsc.org
FSC® C014540

British Library Catalogue in Publishing Data.
A CIP catalogue record for this book is available from the British Library.

CONTENTS

March. 18th. 1860.

Every month shows more strikingly the altered position of Ecclesiastical affairs, & the disposition which exist in the House of Commons to deal with them in an unavailing & rather hostile manner. It is not so many years back that matters connected with the Church were of rare occurrence, of slender interest, & of debateless formality in the Business of the House. But Session by Session we have seen questions creeping into importance, which are of essential consequence

A page from the diary

Introduction

THE PARISH OF Hentland and Hoarwithy lies in the south of the county of Herefordshire, in the area known from Domesday Book as Archenfield. In ancient times, this was an independent Welsh-speaking kingdom, an area of land bounded by the River Wye, the River Monnow and the Worm Brook. Its independency was tolerated by the invading Normans as a useful buffer state between England and Wales.

The name 'Hentland' is derived from the Welsh 'hen-llan', meaning 'the old sacred enclosure', and Hentland Church may occupy one of the most ancient Christian sites in the area. Stories are told of Saint Dyfrig (or Dubricius in Latin, or Devereux to the Normans) to whom this church is dedicated. He was born nearby in the middle of the fifth century as the illegitimate grandson of the king of Archenfield, and when he grew up, he evangelised a wide area of south Herefordshire, founding a seminary at Llanfrother ('the church of the brethren') which lies within the parish, training ministers and missionaries. Later, Dyfrig became bishop of Llandaff, and at his death was buried on Bardsey Island. Many wonderful (and unlikely!) folk-tales have grown up around his story.

Hentland nowadays is a tiny hamlet at the end of half a mile of single-track lane with a pot-holed surface and grass growing down the middle; it comprises just the church with a handful of houses bordering the lane. However, a glance at the Ordnance Survey map

Hentland Church

gives clues to its relative importance in times gone by: at least five green lanes and footpaths converge on the hamlet from all directions, and doubtless in the past it was a much more substantial village.

The parish is long and thin, stretching more or less north-south, with Hentland Church in the south, Hoarwithy Church towards the north and the hamlet of Kynaston in between.

Today, Hoarwithy village is larger than Hentland. Its cottages are confined to the west bank of the River Wye, either built up above the road on the side of the valley, or risking the annual flooding of the river on lower ground by the river bank. There has been a crossing-place of the river here for millennia: first by the ford where the Roman road from Kings Caple meets the river at Red Rail (the unusual name is said to be derived from the Welsh for 'the street of the ford'), and later by ferry and later still by the bridge, first built in 1856.

Hoarwithy Church was originally built in the 1840s, as a chapel-of-ease for parishioners who found the journey from the north of the parish to Hentland Church too arduous. One description of

The original chapel at Hoarwithy

the building was, 'An ugly brick building with no pretensions to any style of architecture'.

This book explains some of the background to how this little chapel changed into the present ornate, Italianate/ Byzantine church: a surprising thing to find in a south Herefordshire village.

Most people who live in Hentland and Hoarwithy have heard of the Revd William Poole, the wealthy nineteenth-century clergyman who planned and paid for the 'beautification' of Hentland and Hoarwithy churches, as well as building a school and a reading room for the villages.

They may also have heard the stories about Poole which have survived for 150 years in the village. It is said that Poole was a difficult, irritable man, not very popular with his parishioners. On one occasion, when the building of Hoarwithy Church was not going to his satisfaction, he was due to pay his workmen at the end of the week. To show his frustration with slow progress and laziness, he stood at the top of the steep path that leads from the church down to the road, and hurled the men's pay, in pennies and half-pennies down the path, so that the men had to grovel in the mud to retrieve it. It seems a sad story to hear about a man of God, and I have often wondered what caused him to be like this, and what sort of man he was.

Towards the end of 2021, I was contacted indirectly by the volunteers who run the Amnesty International bookshop in York. A diary had been donated to the shop, which seemed to have been written by a clergyman in the nineteenth century, and he made mention of Hentland and Hoarwithy. Did I have any information, they asked, as to who he might have been, because they had been reading what they could make out of the diary, and they felt rather sorry for him?

The diary

The dates in the diary gave us an instant answer: the diary belonged to the Reverend William Poole, covering the years between 1857 and 1862. The bookshop was glad to find a home for the diary in return for a donation, and so the little leather-bound book returned to its origins in Herefordshire.

It took a long time to transcribe the diary: Poole's handwriting varies between concise, clear script (once one has got used to the way a double 's' was written at that time), and a wild illegible scrawl, the latter especially when he was feeling emotional, unhappy or in his many prayers. Of course, the diary was not written for anyone to read apart from its author, but still it gives glimpses into Poole's life, his viewpoint, the political situation at the time and Poole's acute sense of duty and responsibility for his parishioners.

I have chosen passages from the diary for this book which I hope may be of general interest, leaving out some of Poole's repetitious self-recrimination about his many failures to fulfil his good intentions.

Besides the diary, it has been possible to look into the history of Poole's family, and to get a feeling for the reasons behind his often depressed mood, and his ever-present awareness of his own mortality. He was born in 1819, the youngest of seven children of extremely wealthy parents, at the family home of Homend, at Stretton Grandison in Herefordshire. Like two of his older brothers, he attended Rugby School from the age of ten, and then went on to Oriel College, Oxford, to read 'Greats' – i.e. Classics. Poole was ordained deacon in All Saints, Hereford in 1844, and ordained priest in 1845.

Poole's oldest sibling was James, who studied law. He married Grace Ann in 1841 but they didn't have any children. They lived at Bisley in Gloucestershire. James died at the early age of 46 in 1857, the year this diary started, and was buried at Bussage, where his widow later entered a convent.

Next was Charlotte, born in 1812. There is no record of her after her birth, and she may have died in infancy. Frances followed in

1813. In 1845 she married James Parson-Hopton, the squire of Dulas Court near Ewyas Harold. They had two daughters and a son, but in 1855, a couple of years before the start of the diary, when this James was 46, they suffered a terrible accident. They were driving a dog cart in Earl Bathurst's park near Cirencester, with a groom in attendance. For some reason the horses became spooked, and the dog cart was overturned with both James and Frances being thrown to the ground. The injured couple were taken home and medical aid was administered, but Captain Hopton had multiple injuries, including a severe head injury, from which he died soon afterwards. Frances Hopton, although seriously hurt, did recover physically, but was dreadfully shocked by the death of her husband. Dulas Court had to be sold, and Frances moved with her children to Cheltenham.

The next child of the family was Edward, born 1814, but he died at the age of just 14 in 1828. Unlike his three brothers, he did not attend Rugby School, so may have been 'delicate' as a child.

Catherine was born in 1815. She never married but continued to live at Homend, caring for her mother after her father's death. Eventually, when her mother died, she went into the 'House of Mercy' convent at Bussage to join her sister-in-law Grace.

Richard was born in 1817. He went to Rugby School like his brothers, and Brasenose College, Oxford in 1836. Later he was admitted to the Middle Temple as a lawyer, but by 1851, in his early 30s, he was in a care home, first in Gloucestershire and later in Portishead, Somerset, where he remained for many years. The census labels him as 'imbecile'. Whether this might have been as the result of a head injury, or mental illness, we don't know. Clearly, he started life with normal intelligence, so there must have been some great tragedy. He lived till the age of 82.

Poole's father died in 1849. So by the time the diary was written, William had lost his father, two brothers and a brother-in-law, and another brother was in care. One sister had died, and all that were left were two sisters and their mother. Wealth was no protection against illness and accident. Life must have seemed very precarious and full of uncertainties to the young William.

A word of explanation: up until the middle of the nineteenth century, Hentland, Little Dewchurch, St Weonards and Llangarron were all chapelries under the umbrella of Lugwardine parish. With the expanding population, it became necessary to elevate former chapelries to parish status. Under the new legislation introduced to facilitate this, the parish priests of new parishes and districts were legally 'perpetual curates'. This was William Poole's title, until 1868 when new legislation was passed which entitled perpetual curates to call themselves 'vicars'.

The Diary
November 1857 — May 1862

1st November, 1857

All Saints Day: the lessons are beautiful and appropriate,
and seem to chime in very harmoniously with the calm decay
of a gently moving autumn, and the softened sorrow which
attaches to the recollections of those whom we this day
celebrate. There is, in the consideration of those already gone
from sight, something that touches so closely on the deepest
sympathies of the heart that we might expect to find both a
shrinking from, and a leaning towards its indulgence. And
that system which has so skilfully seized all the avenues to
the heart has made full use of this, and it is impossible to
read for the first time, and till we have discovered the almost
punning perversion of the application, the verse that stands
at the head of the list of the dead to be prayed for "Have pity
upon me, O ye my friends, for the hand of God has touched
me" without almost a shudder of interest. But call to mind
that it is not the dead in their place of ultimate purgation
who utter these thrilling words, but Job on his dunghill,[I] in
conflict with his friends, and we see at once a 'tour d'adresse',[II]
rather than a solemn application of Scripture.

[I] Job 19.21.
[II] 'feat of skill'.

1

Funeral sermon for Mr Addis about 92, who, as far as I could learn, had not been in church for 36 years.

Kingsford here – letter from Price with bad news – confused accounts of the taking of Delhi.[I]

Thus I begin this volume: O Lord, may it help me, by thy grace, to search and try my ways, to correct faults, and to grow in nearness to Thee. Per JC. Amen.

22nd November, 1857

Two days at Wroxall Abbey[II] with CW Hoskyns. The Abbey stands on the broad watershed of Central England, its streams running to Humber and Severn: and like many rivershead homes, is marked more by the absence of any notable feature, than by the hill or rocky springhead. A broad plain, in recent years common and moorland, now cultivated and divided into well-shaped fields, and lined with strips of plantation, affords every little undulation full opportunity of exhibition, and by taking advantage of the slopes and natural banks, by aiding the height with plantations and duly opening the sweep of the upper combe, certain variety can be obtained. But there are no striking natural features to observe: the abbey is an old building, surrounding a quadrangle, on one side formed by the church, others by the

---

[I] The Indian Mutiny of 1857, of sepoys employed by the British East India Company, resulted in huge loss of life. Delhi was overrun by the rebellion, and it was many months before British reinforcements recovered control of the city.

[II] Wroxall Abbey: family home of the descendents of Sir Christopher Wren, near Solihull.

old building of the nunnery, raised in more recent days, and the fourth a red brick house, with a handsome front and some good rooms but little harmonising with the old arches and buttresses, some of which date back as far as the reign of Stephen. There is great room for architectural occupation which would need a long purse to do satisfactorily. The old church, which is used as a parish church, has much of ornaments, and could be made very good, which in due course of time would be done. The owner leads a life of activity, in local county agriculture. Business very much enjoyed and, thrown by his reputation and talents among men whose minds have received a higher religious tendency, he has imbibed a good deal of this sentiment, and seems to have shaken off any lightness of sentiment which he might have entertained.

20th December, 1857

The year grows old amid mild storm, sunny days, roaring winds and cold fogs, which succeed each other in quick rotation. One single frost has, up to this time, given us the only foretaste of winter, and this after a summer of unusual heat and fineness.

I am fast getting on towards that age when they say that men become accustomed to living alone, and cease to wish for the household voices that chime so sweetly on the imagination of earlier years. I know not whether I shall reach that stage of feeling, or whether I shall come to reach that age, to which I am now drawing near: but I think it is time for me to lay aside, once for all, that repining feeling, which under the complaint of loneliness is too apt to creep over me. If I am alone, it is because I have chosen to lay aside the society which I used to frequent, and keep close to what I called my duty – if it was my duty. Then there is nothing to regret, and if I am so situated as to find in combination with this attention to my Parish no neighbouring mind with whom I love to exchange counsel, surely that is a disposition of events, so beyond my control, as to make acquiescence a simple duty. No, no! It is not in the outward lot that the mischief lies, but in the clumsy way in which I adapt myself to it: in the errors and failings and sins which I do not with strong hand throw out: and suffer them to hang their branches about the avenues of my mind – darkening, shading, and engulfing its fresh air, and shutting out the sweet and healthful sun and breeze of the cheerfulness that springs from the spirit of Jesus.

O blessed Lord, again I pray Thee to give me that bold, hearty determination to walk in thy ways, driving away and putting out the sin that doth so sorely beset me – searching and trying my ways, living thy Word, and seeking thee in continual prayer and practical meditation. Which, all are thy gifts, O blessed Lord – only turned aside and still so much unenjoyed because of my cowardly acquiescence in the approach of evil.

22nd December, 1857

Passed a singular morning. Just before going out I took up Tom Brown,[1] and was led into a kind of attempt to identify

---

[1] *Tom Brown's Schooldays* by Thomas Hughes. Hughes attended Rugby School from 1834 to 1842. William Poole was a pupil there 1829–37.

the characters; in following this I took down the Rugby
registers, and then, partly from the circumstances of the
story, partly from the names, which the register brought
before me, I went back to the whole record of school. The
various phases of that life came before me, mixed up with
strange confusion of times: evidently I confused together
different periods and things which, in their very nature
could only have been of the shortest duration, but appeared
to spread over years; and things that reflection told me must
have been going on daily for years left no mark – had no
memorial in the mind.

Well, school has its indelible record, but when I look back,
I freely own the good which I owe to my school life. I ask
also, what good thing did I do at school? What manly,
straightforward, bold, open, generous upright actions – alas!
How few. Was not selfishness in some form my guiding star
there, and has it not ever since been at my side? Are not those
things which I more clearly recall from school, things in
which my own praise and good name have been embalmed,
and has not the long line of selfishness stained and damaged
not only school life, but the miserable existence of Oxford?
Well. I am thankful that I have lived to see this, and I am
thankful that I have, I trust, a better view of life now, and
I hope that the power of Jesus Christ will enable me to live
in a way more becoming his service – and that when my
schooldays are over, I may be educated for His work.

*I wonder whether William was miserable at Oxford, or whether he is now
regretting normal undergraduate pranks and excesses? We shall never know.*

5

31st December, 1857

Ten minutes before 12.

1857 is almost gone; it has lost its daylight, and the full moon looks down on its passing minutes, mild and quiet and warm as April or October. A stirring year it has been abroad, at home – a year with much to make men feel that we stand in the hand of a higher Ruler. With much to make men afraid, when they see the worldly spirit which animates so many: with much to make them hopeful, when they see that a good seed exists, and think on the exceeding goodness of God shown us in so many ways, and with such merciful circumstances, whether in India, or at home.

But at this hour I would turn to my own private business and look at my preparation for the coming year. Shall I live it out? Who knows? And if I do, how can I best guide myself to God's glory? What are the main points in which I have been traitorous to my high calling? If I do not, what are the things that will most terrify me, when I lie within eyesight of eternity?

1) In public work I have been rather more bustling and hasty, than steady, active and thorough in what I have begun. I have not, I fear, duly considered the claims of my neighbours, and I have been vain and used my employment as food to this vanity. More careful arrangement of time, wiser control over people and things, and more hearty cooperative feeling with those with whom I am called to act, and a more entire clearing of worldly thoughts and aspirations, using the world and not abusing it. Indeed, it is a far higher condition of mind to mix with a variety of worldly matter – business

matters, and not be lowered or secularised by it, than to stand aloof from the worry in the quiet of a convent garden, in the peacefulness of a continual devotion. O blessed Lord, grant me a devoted humble Christian mind in the midst of the troubles and trials of this busy world.

2) Private conduct: to fit me for death: I need a careful discipline of thought, a more regular and continued devotional study of the Bible; earlier rising and a more regular system of self-examination. These, God graciously helping me through the power of Jesus Christ and his Spirit, may bring me to see my faults more clearly, to repent of them more heartily, and to put them away. Oh blessed Lord, grant me a heart to aim at these things honestly and truly, to seek thy Holy Spirit to guide me, to love its fruits and those who hear them: to love thy people, and to show towards them a wise charity and kindness which may keep my heart open to Thee. O give me thyself, the full love of thee, the desire to be in thy presence, by grace now, and to enjoy thy spiritual mercy, now – and to be with thee for ever with all thy saints, when the few years of this anxious chequered life have passed away. Amen, amen.

Now perhaps we come to another of the roots of William's depression and negativity.

31st January, 1858

On Wednesday last, Berkeley Stanhope[I] married Caroline
Arkwright[II] – I have written it quietly like any other words,
I have spoken it coolly like any other fragment of news. It is
well – and necessary to accustom myself to this. May long
years of happiness lie before them – it is my sincere wish.
Him I have known many years, one of the few cases in which
a boyish liking has abided, which in so many cases I have seen
pass away. I have for years been intimate with him, and we
have freely exchanged thoughts and views. There has been
nothing in this to weaken or lower my opinion of him. I would
that it were so with all – that I had not met here with false
professions and promises unfulfilled, with a crookedness of
conduct which must change my opinion and alter my conduct
through life towards one old friend. But indeed, why judge
others and think of others; we have all faults and failings
enough: at home I have enough to look at. My present work,
then, is to fulfil my duty: to look on to nothing of worldly
prospects, contented to let every day open and close, nothing
anticipating, and looking backwards to nothing: no dreams,
no regrets; if the way is opened I will follow it. If closed, I will
sit down at the gate and count the chestnuts that fall from the
tree; only in all, whether of good or evil, of my own sorrow, of

---

[I] Berkeley Lionel Scudamore Stanhope was vicar of Bosbury at this time. In the
1851 census he is noted as perpetual curate of Ballingham. The son of a baronet,
he was 33 at the time of the marriage. Later, he became archdeacon of Hereford.

[II] There is a portrait of Caroline Arkwright in the National Portrait Gallery: https://
www.npg.org.uk/collections/search/portrait/mw150624/Caroline-Sarah-Stanhope-
ne-Arkwright. It shows an elegant, handsome woman in elaborate Victorian
dress. She was the oldest daughter of John Arkwright, magistrate, of Hope-under
Dinmore. Doubtless William, Caroline and Stanhope would all have moved in the
same social circles and known each other a long time.

loneliness or company of society or solitude, let the guiding ruling and prevailing thought be to do thy will, O God, and walk in thy ways: to seek ever more and more to be in the mystical union and spiritual life with Jesus Christ, my blessed Lord and compassionate Saviour. Amen.

18th March, 1858

Two months without a record, sure sign of slothfulness in my work, or of the indisposition which causes sloth. Here, perhaps, a little of both. And now I have reached a time of life when the novelty and interest are in great measure gone by, when most people have shrunk into the cell of family affections and are kept with all their feelings fresh and tender, in the circle of the family fireside. I am still living, as was well perhaps for a young man – as may no doubt be well for me – but still with a demand for especial care. The solitary life, the hired house, the unsettled position and the excitement which carried off these things now gone by. The constant tendency to wish things otherwise. The thoughts of abandoning the place, and the discontent at my deceived expectations – these things need a sure and firm hand of correction. If I am to go – go. If I am to stay – stay; when the time for judging comes it can be soon settled, but neither going or staying should there be any wavering or discontent. Above all there should be no slackness in the work such as now grows over me, while I work and wish and expect and plan, and may not men in this interval be driven into evil ways, and bad habits strengthened, and ill feelings generated and confirmed, which a little unrelaxed attention might have gone far to cure.

Dulas sale tomorrow: over yesterday, looking at the goods; strange collection of things valuable and trashy, but all old and quaint, which it was the pride and pleasure of their master to put together, ever expecting that among them some treasure would come to light which would repay him tenfold for his outlay, and so he went on, hoping without ground, and meanwhile living on borrowed money; buying on borrowed capital and eating up his income with interest. And so amidst all his schemes, getting more and more involved, his health failing, his resources drying up, he died and left his wife and family with scarce money enough to live: save that her fortune was safely secured, all would have been swallowed up and the creditors left unpaid. So Chancery steps in, and the sale takes place tomorrow, and the quaint old odds and ends, brought together with infinite pains and trouble during a quarter of a century, will again be dispersed unto as many places as those from which they were got together.

And so we hear the continuation of the unhappy story of William's sister Frances and her husband, James Parson-Hopton of Dulas Court. James died intestate in 1855. There had been a farm sale in 1853 of livestock, machinery and carriages: a

sign that James was already in financial difficulty. The estate was sold after his
death in 1857, and the furniture went in 1858. It was just as well for Frances that
her own family had made sure that she was financially secure. She moved away to
the Cheltenham area with her three children.

16th May, 1858

Again two months. Two records in four months – either the
good of these notices is found to be little, or I have failed in
accomplishing a good. A month of influenza, still in modified
form, hanging on and making my work a labour, and excusing
where excuses are least needed.

The world during these months has been politically astir,
seeing Palmerston replaced by Lord Derby,[1] and now already
this latter wavering in his new seat. Nothing strikes so much
as the want of leading characters among the public men of
this day; clever men there are few. Respectable men in large
proportion, men of high moral and religious feeling may be
found, but that combination of talents and knowledge with a
fixed purpose and a resolute determination, which we sum up
in the phrase 'great character' – is utterly and entirely absent.
Few they have always been in history – the Richelieus,
Alberonis, Straffords, Wolseys, Frederics, Raffles, Burleighs,
Mirabeaus, Potenkins, (I have purposely joined together
these apparently incongruous specimens as all more or less
showing the quality of which I am thinking) appear only
from time to time.

---

[1] Henry John Temple, 3rd Viscount Palmerston, successively Tory, Whig, Liberal,
prime minister 1855-58. Lord Edward Smith-Stanley, 14th Earl of Derby,
conservative, prime minister from 1858.

Society, during the long level of its annals, blunders on from year to year; the great compensation of Nature making itself evident in this, by the mistakes and errors of one man neutralising the follies of another, and thus actually producing, through the double negation of folly, the fruits of practical wisdom. Thus we stand today in a position of extreme second-ratedness, the North ministry[I] hardly ruling a country with less command of talent than is now at the disposal of any Muntz-framing[II] individual: deduct Pitt and his father from the latter half of the last century and what great names shall we find among leading ministers? Burke held a subordinate position, the fruit of the £30,000; deduct Walpole from the earlier portion and how large a field of mediocrity is presented in the ministries of England. It is so noble a sight to see the actions of a great man passing under our eyes, to hear his words influencing audiences and guiding public opinion, to have his firm and sound judgement to lean on in every critical emergency, and to find this judgement delivered in clear, decided language, and fortified by sound, comprehensible reasoning, that I suppose it is unreasonable to expect this enjoyment twice within the compass of a lifetime. They who have been witnesses of a portion of the lives of Wellington[III] and Peel[IV] must not be disappointed if their lot calls them to run out the remainder of their days among the murmurs of conscious

---

[I] Lord North, prime minister of Britain 1770–82 during the American War of Independence.

[II] George Frederick Muntz: Liberal MP for Birmingham. Industrialist, opponent of church rates.

[III] Arthur Wellesley, 1st Duke of Wellington. Field marshal and prime minister 1828–30.

[IV] Sir Robert Peel, 2nd Baronet, prime minister 1841–6.

incompetency; and the restless complaints of a people whose general intelligence has run more closely than is usual or convenient on the foolishness of their most prominent politicians.

Church Rates[1] seem to be abandoned in the House of Commons and the Church in no way prepared to supply the deficiency, with no plan proposed, no general scheme even suggested.

23rd May, 1858

Whit Sunday, stormy and cold: poor congregation in the morning, good in the afternoon, 16 communicants.

Lord enable me by thy grace to carry out the purposes of my heart, avowed before thee this day.

Very small congregations in the country parishes of the Church of England in the mid-nineteenth century were evidently just as common as they are in the twenty-first century!

Intensely critical of others though Poole was, he was no less critical of himself, as we read over and over again.

---

[1] Church rates: the church rate was a tax formerly levied in each parish in England and Ireland for the benefit of the parish church. The rates were used to meet the costs of carrying on divine service, repairing the fabric of the church and paying the salaries of the connected officials.

11th July, 1858

Three services on the Sunday, and on arrival at home at 9pm, have furnished arguments against any Sunday evening notices: and on other days the long warm evenings have enticed me into late wanderings, and the various occupations by which I have been encircled have prevented the record on other days; and yet, look at Charles Napier:[1] among all the business of Indian Command, writing full and minute statements on almost every event that occurred. True, he had a serious and stirring theme, and he had the zeal and courage of ten men to face his labours.

Quiet in the world: stagnation in activity, perhaps, is the danger most likely to injure me. Lazy altogether I am not now, I hope, in danger of becoming, but to let personal activity take the place of spiritual work would be a traitorous abandonment of my especial function. Let me beware then of this snare. Society: visiting etc, I have pretty well put aside. The other is now to be watched.

At the advanced age of 38, William ponders on the difficulties of finding friends:

15th August, 1858

As youthfulness drops off and the man finds himself insensibly reckoned no more among the young, but among those whose years are well advanced, certain changes in the conduct of life become evidently forced upon him. He can no

---

[1] Sir Charles James Napier, Commander-in-Chief of India 1848–9.

longer class himself with the body of light-hearted youngsters who, every year, take their place in the circle of life. They shrink from him as an old fellow, who would be too grave for their age, or who would ill assume the ways and manner so natural, they suppose, to themselves. So they feel a certain half-respectful unwillingness to enter in his society, with all the lightness of their years. They associate with him; perhaps they feel it is a compliment to be associated with him, but it is not as on equal terms, as one companion with another. It is rather as a check to the words and freedom which they enjoy. He cannot then see any more races rise up in terms of almost friendship to pass on and leave him in the lurch, as the engagements, position, associations of life lead them onwards on their different ways. Now where then shall this man of growing age find his resource? The natural and happiest lot is to find the daily companionship in married life, and to exchange then on equal terms with your fellows the lighter companionship which is not all your society. But if this be denied, then the association of a few of like age and kindred pursuits, if such can be found in like situation with himself. For always there is a sort of inequality between the friendship of the single and married man; to one, his friend is a valued and real blessing: he would do as much for him as any – but to the single man, it is his all. His fate, by which the affections pass in and out and pass their daily play – then if 2 or 3 of like situation and taste continue through life within reach of each other, there the danger is overcome of those selfish and narrow-minded ways arising in the heart, which the commonsense of mankind has agreed to condemn by the not foolish denomination of Old Bachelorism.

Poole paints a picture of his parishioners enjoying a special day. It tells us a good deal about the class structure of the nineteenth century, and William's attitude to his own place in it:

29th September, 1858

A Harvest Festival and school opening at Whitchurch.
Service in the morning at 11am.
Sermon by Archdeacon Freer.
Lunch at 1pm. Dinner for labourers in separate tent.
Presentation of Testimonial to Powles by Blakemore.
Games and Sports.

Dinner to all the farmers' labourers and the parents of children at school, with a ticket for drink (2 pints for men, 1 pint for women) and a payment for admittance into the field. When rain came about 6pm, it had been very successful. Sports chiefly races: sacks, buckets and hurdle races about the best received. The women running was an offence to me. Throwing the hammer was rather dull, the greased pole not successful from being too large. Race backwards was amusing. Dined with the labourers and found them very well behaved, and full, as usual, of their own humour, and with one exception, most seemed to be quite contented. The conclusions are:

1) that these feasts need at present a large infusion of influential gentry to make them go off as they should. The farmer is too aristocratic, and not yet accustomed to consult the concurrence of his men, as gentlemen do that of their servants. They should have dined in one large tent, but while the farmers had the management, this was quite out of the question. Yet

it promoted good feeling in them. They were pleased with themselves, and so with their men. The men were happy, but the thing is yet too new to be quite thoroughly entered into. One woman was exceedingly wrath with her boy for running in sacks, and with me for taking his part.

2) That it is not wise to try them as yet, except in very favourable circumstances and in scattered localities, i.e. here and there in a district, that their successful issue there may strengthen people's hands.

3) Where they are tried, the sports should be very well rehearsed, and quickly following one another, and the keepers of the course should be firm, good-humoured and active.

4) That the different orders should take part in it, and that athletic sports should make as much as possible a part, where there is credit in winning; sports which would show that a man was likely to be an able workman.

In spite of some of these canons not being perfectly fulfilled today, yet the affair was successful, and I hope came to an end in quiet.

They sought the praise of men more than the praise of God. Not to think of themselves higher than they ought to think.

Let me bear this ever in mind. Help me, O Lord, to be humble, honest, pure, diligent and attentive.
Per JC. Amen.

Poor William continues his theme of self-pity and loneliness:

10th October, 1858

My birthday, and I am now 39. God orders our ways in his wisdom; in my thoughts I little expected to be living a solitary bachelor at this age. I had drawn my charming picture of a parsonage, modest yet graceful, attractive more by the taste of its appurtenances and the welcome of its owners, than by luxury or wealth displayed there; and I had crowned this refined home by a vision of purity 'not too good for human nature's daily food', where religion was mixed with sense and spirit, and that grace that springs from a good disposition and a Christian education. And here I pictured rest at home amid increasing outward toil, here 'unhasting, unresting diligence', was to find its support and encouragement, its repose and relaxation, and here, in the Valley of Home, soothed by the sweet sounds and lovely sights which cluster around that fairest and most precious nook in the 'wilderness of this life', I looked to pass gently onward to an age of gradual decline amid 'all that should accompany old age', till I passed as a ripe shock[1] to a better world.

Yet how much of selfishness, how much of vanity created and cherished this little page of romance? Well for me, I would

---

[1] Job 5.26.

believe, that these 'sheltering bowers' have all been 'rent'. Well for me, I would hope, that I stand now on my 39th birthday, a lonely hanger-on on society, lodging in a 'wee bit cot', with no home that I can call my own. Well for me, all this, certainly, if I can read in it the correction of past errors, and make it do duty for what it was appointed. [*Followed by long prayer.*]

14th November, 1858

Cold sharp frosts, with a keen easterly wind and bright sunshine have kept up the credit of St Martin this year.[I] A run with Price, for one night to Bussage,[II] where all seems to run on with even flow of activity: a little perhaps of the influence which Suckling carried with him and left behind him.

Letter from Bishop (Hampden)[III] about Bridstow, in which he says he makes it a rule to consider not the person's situation who may take a living, but the needs and requirements of the parish, independent of helping and aiding a deserving clergyman. How then are poor clergymen to get

---

[I] 'St Martin's summer' is an old term for a brief sunny spell around this date: the feast day of St Martin of Tours is November 11th.

[II] Bussage is a village near Stroud. In 1844, a new church was built there, sponsored by members of the Oxford Movement. It was to be 'substantial, beautiful, and handsomely adorned', and was dedicated to St Michael and All Angels. The first vicar of Bussage was the Revd Robert Suckling. A few years later, the Bussage House of Mercy was started. Houses of Mercy were Anglican institutions set up to house 'fallen women', who were often simply unmarried mothers, or sometimes sex workers. They were given the necessary training to find jobs as domestic servants. Grace Anne Poole, William's widowed sister-in-law, was the first Mother Superior. Bussage House of Mercy housed 26 girls aged 14–18 years.

[III] Renn Dickson Hampden, Bishop of Hereford 1848–68. Liberal: at odds with the Oxford movement.

on? What encouragement will there be for hard-working poverty and patient endurance of trial, if riches are thought necessary to the holding of a moderate living?

Booker-Blakemore's[I] death has taken the world by surprise – seen in the Strand on Saturday by W H Cooke, in perfect heath, died at Kingston of apoplexy on Sunday, leaving our country the legacy of an election. A kind-hearted man, but his outward profession of churchism and high principle hung awkwardly on one whose private life was so little in accordance with it.

12th December, 1858

On 30th November to Lea's at Droitwich, where I preached: saw John Lea about my Will, felt poorly, came back next day to Diocesan Board meeting. Went on to Whitfield, and from there next day to Homend, and so home on Friday, intending to give the next fortnight or 3 weeks to hard parish work. But we see only the skeleton of things, and the fashioning of the full frame lies not in us. On Saturday I had a sort of grumbling pain: it might be indigestion, it might be nothing. On Saturday evening, while looking in at Tretire, it grew worse, and well-dosed with vile Tinc Rhub[II] to no effect. After visiting a few people at Chapel Tump, I caught a wetting on my way down to Hoarwithy, where I suffered as severe a pain as ever I felt. By eight at home and in bed, but

---

[I] Thomas Booker-Blakemore, MP for Herefordshire 1819–58: industrialist, very wealthy.

[II] Tincture of Rhubarb, made from the rhizome, used as a laxative for digestive problems.

pain lasted, and now the Sunday week following, I begin to feel more of ancient vigour than for many weeks past, though by very plain tokens I know and feel that I am far from health. I thank God for my recovery, and I would pray that I may profit really and substantially by the lesson. A whole week, from Saturday night till Sunday, from 4th to 12th December, either wholly spent in bed and room, or at most, on 2 or 3 days varied with an hour's stroll in the garden, etc.

19th December, 1858

A week of slow but continued amendment, which has brought me to daily exercise out of doors, and has suffered me to go through the usual Sunday services, by the help of driving and taking care of myself. This week, if no relapse takes place, I may hope to go about my parish again, redeeming the time, by God's mercy.

26th December, 1858

Christmas is come and gone. Wet and gloomy: as ever, dulled the more genial feelings which belong to it by prescription.

A more gradual amendment than I had hoped has made this week also useless for any parish work, and I still feel enough of the remnants of illness about me to make me feel very uncertain about the future.

The Christmas Communion few, both from the wet and from my long inability to do as I had hoped in arguing with the backward. May I be careful not to lose any opportunities that may hereafter be given me. But though few in number, its use, its blessing was not weakened. May I profit and not throw away the grace by sloth, folly, negligence, indulgence.

31st December, 1858

Ten minutes before 12 o'clock. Again on the confines of a dying year, and thought runs backward over the 12 months past, and finds, I fear, a tale that is not of continued advance and growth. Disappointment has weighed very heavily upon me, when indeed it should by this time have lost all sting, and have produced the peaceable fruits of righteousness, and why has it not? Partly because I have not laboured to root out the clogging sins, and to bring myself to that sweet and glad acquiescence in the will of God: what the Christian finds to be the sufficient recompense for any and all griefs. Partly that I have not determined with all strength of will to fix my hopes, by full and more daily exercise of anticipation not on any earthly future, but on that 'eternal life', which in reality and to true faith so far outbalances this. O Lord, give me grace to feel, to believe, to act on this truth; to seek that joy that fadeth not away, and from the ashes of earthly dreams, wisely, I believe: kindly, lovingly consumed, to assume that higher, holier, more unvarying joy which rests on the right hand on high. [*Followed by prayer.*]

13th February, 1859

Another link broken, another of those who have been joined to my circle of relations has been called off; and I have seen Maria Hopton laid where so many of her name have been before placed, in the vault of the little church at Canon Frome. The petted child of wealth, she bore in her somewhat showy and attractive manners the marks of early indulgence: a little of the waywardness of the spoiled child of fortune might be seen now and then in her doings. But she made a most domestic companion to John Hopton, whose life became from the date of his marriage more entirely altered and rearranged than commonly happens to a man of fixed pursuits and rather decided will. Her favourite daughter Mabel, intellectual, with feelings and ways not perhaps readily understood, died about ten months ago, leaving a void in her mother's heart, and a sadness on her life, and a weakness in her health which did not survive another confinement, in which, taking the infection of scarletina, according to the almost universal laws of nature, she sunk under the weakness and the disease. It has this especial warning to me – that she was of my age precisely, and she, in mid-life with friends and family, with wealth and enjoyments, has so passed away, her work worked out. What is there to make a matter of surprise if I too, in like manner, be called off, leaving the record of many unfinished deeds, of imperfection in those that have been attempted, and of a long consciousness of many amendments which should be and which have not been effected. I have meant much, tried a little and thoroughly carried out nothing. Well might those great minds of Strafford[I] and Laud[II] make 'thorough' the sign and test of greatness in their work. If, however it may clash with varying convictions and a determination to keep well with all parties, yet for satisfaction, for effect, for usefulness, for whatever writes its character on the history of nations or churches, or schools of philosophy, or more private institutions, he must work to what is thoroughly considered and thoroughly done. May I, weak waverer, receive that help per extero[III] which will enable me to be thorough at least in the main points, and through the influence of 'one thing accomplished', carry on the thoroughness into all branches of life, so long as I am suffered to remain here.

Evidently William continued to feel under the weather, following whatever it was that afflicted him back in early December, perhaps accentuated by the illness and death of those around him.

[I] Thomas Wentworth, 1st earl of Strafford, English statesman, supporter of Charles I. Executed during the Civil War.

[II] William Laud, Archbishop of Canterbury under Charles I. An advocate of high church ritualism. Executed during the Civil War.

[III] from outside.

6th March, 1859

I am gradually reaching the conviction that my present work is more than I can satisfactorily perform. For some months now, I have been toiling after it, in the vain hope of overtaking it, and with the dull, hopeless feeling of leaving some part still unaccomplished. If I was in the full vigour of health, and with the freshness of zeal which would carry me on, there would not, I think, be more than should be duly attended to. But then I must learn to make use of the early morning and the evening hours for other purposes than relaxation: and if I must be on a sofa, or read only books of amusement or light literature in the evening, much must be necessarily hurried over. Illness, it is true, has left its mark, and that has not been followed by any thorough and complete change which might give tone to the system, and show whether it were really or no the failing of the powers of the body, or only the lingerings of ill-health, temporary in themselves, and only permanent because they have not had the door held open for them to march out at leisure.

An expedition gave William something more to think about in the wider world:

Since my last record, I have been to Oxford, where I came in contact with Stanley, Shepherd, Rawlinson, Chase, Chretien, etc, and hoped or fancied that something of a more manly tone was becoming not unusual among the men – in spite of peg-tops[I] and side-holders. While among the 'Dons', I seemed

---

[I] Peg-top trousers: these trousers had an abundance of material at the hips, which gave a baggy look. Pleats and panels allowed the trouser legs to narrow dramatically to a close-fitting hem at the ankle.

to observe an absence of that fresh, hopeful spirit which is the accompaniment, and perhaps the cause, of almost all successful work. They had too, not the sneering spirit which I remember some years back, in Froude[I] and his fellow fellows at Exeter – and which issued so disastrously – but a sort of readiness to despise all the protections and regulations of the former generation, and to enter on a contest with other factions of the world in a spirit of perfect equality, on terms of no advantage to either side. A way of action which the English church and universities, by their constitutions and doctrines, most admirably suited to excel in; if their members were trained to such contest, and, either in worldly wisdom or unity of feeling in Christian self-denial, fitted to compete with all the most practised gladiators of the hostile armies of the religion.

Poole evidently had problems in communicating with the working class men in his parish, despite his best efforts.

Sacrament at Hentland – no labouring men. 'O fortunatos nimium sua si bona norint, agricolas'.[II] But how to teach them? May I have patient, hopeful, watchful zeal to look into their hearts one by one, never flagging, never hasting, never giving up – above all, never thinking mere consumption of time in parish work is the full demand of the Parish System. It is not only time spent, but well spent – not only talk, but spiritual talk; not only outward but real soul-reaching ministrations that satisfy the vow of ordination. Lord, enable me to do this, with honesty, activity and patience.

[I] James Anthony Froude, fellow of Exeter College, Oxford. Controversial opponent of the Oxford Movement.

[II] 'The farmers would count themselves lucky, if they only knew how good they had it' (Virgil).

3rd April, 1859

I have been, a week back, to Barnard Castle ? miles – twelve
hours by railway, through the whole length of England,
and this traversed twice without impediment, without a
disagreeable occurrence: not an uncivil word, or angry look, or
impatient gesture, or unwilling compliance, or ill-mannered
behaviour to interfere with the ease of the journey. What
a marvel of comfort – what a change from the old coach
system, when every stage brought its irritating dispute, its
surly acceptance of the too small gifts: its cursing at hostlers
or horses, its more than idle tales, its over-abundant beer-
drinking, its discomfort and annoyances. But has this change
had any effect upon the character of the people? Certainly it
cannot be so universally spread without indicating something
more of consideration of the wants and conveniences of others,
than existed under the old scheme. But the danger is that this
outward comfort and mannerism will satisfy a large portion of
people altogether, who will never come to search deeper and
further into the springs of happiness.

Hoarwithy bridge, with the toll-house

Still poorly, but the cold shaken off a good deal, but the cough lingers still.

Poor William – talk about a glass half-empty personality!

The first timber bridge at Hoarwithy was built in 1856, shortly before the period covered by the diary. Before this there was just the ford or ferry. The new bridge would suddenly have opened up the villages to the east for the people of Hoarwithy.

The Ross to Hereford railway opened in 1855, shortly after Poole arrived in Hentland. Presumably he would have travelled down from Kynaston to Fawley station by pony and trap, as Ballingham station and Backney Halt had not yet been opened. It must have been life-changing for people who, like Poole, could afford the train. There is a delightful account of the opening of the new railway at: https://htt.herefordshire.gov.uk/herefordshires-past/the-post-medieval-period/ transport/railways/the-opening-of-the-herefordshire-railways/the-hereford-ross-and-gloucester-railway/

Etherege has left – alas! How I have been deceived – false utterly – a thief – drunken once at least – and several times at the public house. And this not told me by James, who was bound to tell me, or by Gunter and his wife, who in reason should have told me.

10th April, 1859

Wrote to Etherege – 11th company, 1st battalion, 9th depot Limerick. May God bless the words to his guidance and correction, that he may be a steady and Christian lad, and if his faults are owing to my doings or neglectings, O Lord, pardon me for Jesus Christ's sake, and hear my prayers for his conversion, unworthy though I be to offer them.

It sounds as if Etherege was one of Poole's servants; he seems to have run as far away from Hentland as possible! His misdeeds are obviously a great disappointment to Poole.

29th May, 1859

Fifth Sunday after Easter. On this Sunday 5 years back I entered on my duties at Hentland, and once only have been absent for two Sundays together since that time, when in the early summer of the year before last, I took a tour of a fortnight with Fanny to Paris, Coblentz and Brussels. I have been in a state of continual expectancy and transition, as I was always expecting and endeavouring to arrange for the building of a Parsonage house, which now at last seems fairly under way. But the school is still unsettled, as no site altogether suitable has hitherto been found. Meanwhile, nothing has been done at Little Dewchurch, and if I were to leave the parish, it would be as yet very much in the same state as I found it in. A parsonage at Hentland, a school and vestry for the same part of the parish, a vestry at Hoarwithy and Little Dewchurch – a clergyman's house and a school at the same place and a sort of school-chapel in conjunction with Goodrich, Peterstow and Bridstow at Glewstone are needed, all of them to put this parish in the same state of ecclesiastical propriety as an ordinarily well-appointed parish. I hope to accomplish some of it: if I am spared and have strength and spirit to continue in the rather trying work which the size and inconvenience of the parish bring with them.

25th July, 1859

Three days in London, which, with a companion, I should have enjoyed, but alone bore with moderate equanimity. The wide, wide wilderness; physically and morally, how strangely it stands in the midst of our little Kingdom – itself a kingdom of its own.

Library of British Museum, Kew Gardens, Battersea, Kensington, All Saints Church, Margaret Street,[1] the finest decoration I have seen. The paleness of the lower part of the east side, consisting of pure alabaster, seemed too weak to

---

[1] All Saints Church, Margaret Street, London: an eighteenth-century chapel remodelled in high Victorian Gothic style by William Butterfield to be an Anglo-Catholic church, consecrated in May, 1859. The church even now will only accept priests who are male, and ordained by a male bishop. If you look at the pictures of the church, you will see where Poole got some of his ideas for Hoarwithy.

support the rich figures and setting which stand over them. The panels of the roof very beautiful, but injured by too free a use of gilding. The pulpit of inlaid marbles: here and there, patches of brickwork appear in strange discord, unlike those in Battersea College chapel, which harmonise with the rougher fabric. The bricks in English, Flemish and other bond.

14th August, 1859

The extreme heat that marked the month of July has passed away, and August has brought for the harvest a cooler season, mixed with rain and sunshine, but at present without damage to the crops. They seem more likely to suffer from the scarceness of hands, which compels ripe crops to be left in the ground and sets farmers fighting for men. I remember 12 or 13 years ago when such a circumstance as scarceness of labourers seemed a contingency almost beyond the bounds of possibility in this part of the country, and the object of everyone was to find anything for people to do. Now, by the common perversity of our nature, many works in many places seem to be waiting only because 'hands' are scarce, and if they were plentiful as of yore, many a goodly undertaking would be entered on.

Charles Hilling was a clever, mischievous lad, who a little older than some of the other boys would sometimes look in on the Sunday School to show his learning and his love of mischief. He went off to learn the blacksmith's trade, and at Jeffry's, at Carey, at Harewood End, etc, etc, I heard of him rather idle, very drunken and pugnacious. Last week taken ill, he came home, they sent for the doctor, found he had brain fever, and after a few days of insensibility he died and was buried on Friday in Hoarwithy churchyard. Some thoughts at last he had – he asked whether they thought he could be saved – and he prayed often in his mother's opinion: but they never sent to me to see him, and I heard of his illness only when it was over, and though it might be little that I could have done, still I should have been glad to have seen him while the sense was still light, and the sense of doubt and danger fanning it – words neglected before might have been listened to. O Lord, lay not to my charge whatever, through my lack of zeal or skill, may have happened to the injury of this poor lad.

5th September, 1859

A ten days absence at Barnard Castle on railway business, varied by certain 'eccentric' wanderings.

At Birmingham to see Weller, and found him from home; at York Habback, and Herbert (Killarney), at Barnard Castle, to Scarth, (Bathwick), to Redcar for Sunday – Postlethwaite

and Milbourne – Camp meeting – Hedlam – Brough,
Penrith – Pooley Bridge. Stormy journey across the Lakes
– to Patterdale late at night – over Kirkstone in a roaring
wind and driving rain. Walk to Fox Home. Mrs Arnold
out – found Ryman Water and Red Bank – over from
Cookson's farm to Brown's hotel, Grasmere – up Helvellyn –
by Langdale – Dungeon Ghyle, Blea Tarn, Chirk, Skelwith,
Clappersgate to Ambleside – by Roch to Windermere: from
Windermere to Hereford leaving at 6.35 and arriving at 3.

I went, ill with cold – toothache, weakness and general out
of sortness; I have returned in fresh health and spirits, thank
God, and with a hope to set to work, within and without, in
good earnest.

11th September, 1859

Glorious day, clear, bright sunshine, golden in its light, rich
with white, silky clouds that sailed over the face of the sun,
and shed a warm, gentle shadow on the yellow stubble, and
woods still summer-green, while a fresh, bracing wind from
the North made exertion a pleasure, and prevented any
approach to the heat and languor of summer. The world after
harvest looks with the self-approval of a lady that has added
to the population of England: a sort of cackling modesty
seems to overlie it all. 'There! See what I have done – how
many mouths have I fed, how many fortunes have I made
– how many ricks are piled up and thatched safe against
all weathers: how many barns and granaries full even to
bursting, and all with the result of my fertile gestation. I can
let the pigs and the geese and the little children rout about

now in my most precious plains, up and down my most sacred enclosures, where a few weeks ago profane steps had caused a tremor and a wrath in all my tenderest ganglions.'

Mother Earth is the lady in happy exhaustion, with her first-born on her arm; we can admire and indulge and praise and pet and flatter her. Yet her labours are not all over – she has the orchard to ripen for the Mill, the hops to dry for the vats, the acorns to mellow for the coarse herd that shall soon be pushing their brazen fronts in every gap and opening where incautious hedger has left the faintest invitation. Alas! for too confident spinsters reposing on the assurance of old Thomas that the garden hedge is 'as good as her can be', and 'nowt can be a-routing through it, leastaways if it's bin now beyond natur.' For hardly shall her gentle steps have gone pattering up the stone steps from the gate, carrying the little basket so well known at the doors of the sick, hardly shall she have got over the rocky roadway at the corner and turned by the old roofless barn into the level winding terrace, when the elements of catastrophe arise on the eye. That quiet look of satisfied contemplation would soon be cast aside with which she gathers in a single glance the soft running river, seen through the boughs at her feet, the rich green meadow sward, dotted with old elms, the remnant of some park-like ground, which once gave dignity to a squire's family, now lost, or worn out or transferred to other homes; the wavy lines of well-cultured fields rising in various height, and with different slopes to the maze of uplands beyond. The rich lines of oak woods climbing up to the very summit of the higher hills, and displaying a jagged edge of foliage against the clear blue sky, while here and there is far-off blue – some point or line of distance, lets out the sympathies to other regions and reminded her that with all its self-contained completeness, even this must be linked by physical as by moral influences with people and lands of a different aspect. If that peaceful, contemplative look could now rest on her little homestead, so tenderly guarded, so diligently cherished, and see that unsightly snout, with many a half-uttered apoplectic grunt, with many a thorn-wrung squeak, yet prevailing more and more upon the pitching quick – developing with awful graduality on the clear space within. First the ring, then the legs, then the cheeks, then the eyes, then with many a toss and jerk, first one ear and then the other. Then with earthquake commotion, which seems to derange the strata of a peark[1] or two of fencing, now up,

now down, now right, now left, comes something of ominous shape – actually a foreleg, quickly followed by another – and then all barriers are broken, all regard of property is despised, the mud-loving animal waddles into the sacred enclosure as contentedly as if her life were needed by the genius that presides over the sacred grove – as confidently as if the delicate graces which years of labour had attached to that little nook were only to be secured by the presence of such a victim.

[1] Wooden frame.

I think this is the most interesting of Poole's diary entries, because it is in such a different mood to the rest: amusing, lyrical, entertaining. Whether it was just that his holiday had done him good, or whether it reveals a tendency to moods which could swing overly high as well as depressingly low, we can only guess. I do think he might have stirred himself to rescue his poor neighbour's garden from the invading pig though!

15th September, 1859

From Whitfield. Senior and his daughter.[1] A man of talent, certainly, and with a knowledge of his talents, but without the least shade of high, ennobling thought: no sacrifice of Roman type will ever be laid by him on the altar of his country. Under the notion of repudiating asceticism, he denounces, I find, all self denial, allows no end to good, and confines this exchange of present and future to the horizon of the present world, so that to hear what we do not like, in hope of becoming fitter for the other life, is not within the scope of his philosophy. He lives much with men of high reputation – Lord Lansdowne, Fitzwilliam, J Bussel and all of the Whig clique, and seems to have the touch and go of conversation which long use of such society may naturally be expected to give. He passes 3 months or more of the year in going from house to house, 3 or 4 days at each, and thus overruns a district of England, and the blank portion of the autumn. He writes a journal of every year – a visit to Ireland, Paris etc, and this is read in MS, and is curious as containing the opinions of the men of name who come in his way, as

---

[1] I think this must be the Revd Archer Clive of Whitfield Court at Wormbridge, and his daughter. It is surprising to us nowadays to find how cosmopolitan society could be in 1859.

he carries introductions to the best. He spoke of the Duc d'Aurunde as a man of remarkable talent and character who seems to wish now to become simply an English gentleman. The Prince of Paris,[I] a fine and promising lad. The others were less favourably described.

Senior is one of the Education Commission and having known nothing of the matter is now diligently getting up the case, and pumping me at all times for my modicum of experience. Seems in favour of a Rating plan, and assisting Diocesan Inspector, and inspecting all schools, public, private, high and low.

Miss Hobhouses – sisters of the Bishop of Nelson[II] – where coals are £3/10 per ton, and where the prices of nearly all articles vary with the arrival of each ship. I had no opportunity of finding out anything relating to the diocese, as I only knew of the relationship at the very end of my visit. Miss Tollet from Bettws, Miss Clive, daughter of archdeacon Clive of Welshpool, and Broadwood and his wife, once Miss Turner – born at Constantinople, and brought up in S America – Captain Yorke.

I have been out so little lately that the society and conversation was like a cordial, and I hope it has not indisposed me for my work here. Whether it will not foster my prevailing faults I will not yet say.

[I] Prince Philippe of Orléans, Count of Paris.
[II] Edmund Hobhouse, Bishop of Nelson, New Zealand 1858–65.

18th September, 1859

Yesterday a Schoolmaster's dinner: about 70 clergy, masters and mistresses – followed by discussion on reading and spelling, and on discipline and tone in schools. The discussion a little languished. Phillott began by laying down the axiom that good reading depended on the grammatical division of the sentences. Clive followed by showing the necessity of considering the occasion and propriety of what was said – and then the matter diverged – but of the masters, only Easton and Bullock took any prominent part. Jackson read a paper on discipline, showing how good discipline lay at the roots of all teaching, and that the bodily as well as mental discipline told, and introduced an enthetical declaration that schoolmasters should leave doctrine to the teachers of doctrine – i.e. the clergymen. Even this did not evoke the masters, but Waring, Hill, with cheese etc, made out the time, and they separated, pleased as it appeared with their meeting.

National Schools were founded in England and Wales during the nineteenth century, by the National Society for promoting Religious Education. The schools provided elementary education, in accordance with the teaching of the Church of England, to the children of the poor. At the time of the 1861 Census, there was a National School in Hoarwithy. The certificated teacher was William Wallis, 21, with Henry Preece, a pupil teacher, aged 14, both of whom lodged with the stonemason in the village. Also recorded as teachers are Mary Anne Bridstow, a 31-year-old widow, who lodged with a farm labourer's family, while her 8-year-old daughter lived with her grandparents in the village, and Anne Steed, aged 63, living with her shoemaker husband. Poole did not build Hentland School till the following year, so I wonder which building was the National School?

Today the rapid falling of night, and the lengthening service of a christening, made it expedient to omit the sermon, and to give notice that the evening service should not be continued. It has lasted since Trinity Sunday, with what results? The congregations have not been as the first and second years' were. The Chapel Tump children never came, and many of the grown up people were absent. The Hoarwithy people seem to hang with a less close connection on Hentland. The singing and more frequent services make them perhaps feel more like a separate parish, but the ill result is that they don't come as they did to the evening service. So much for the externals of it. In the inner part – I have lectured on the articles of the Creed – with what profit to those who heard, God only knows: with what hindrance to success in my own vanity or sloth I may too well suspect. [*Followed by prayer.*]

21st September, 1859

To Stretton,[1] to dinner. Upton Richards, of All Saints, Margaret Street, now quite white, which in contrast to his dark, lively eyes gives the appearance of energy, and perhaps also of humour; he seems a very amiable, good-humoured man, with a sense of the ludicrous, and a firm determination to hold to his own views – but not, I should say, with much fertility of invention, or originality of thought, but from his steadiness, firmness and good sense, deserves as he professes the confidence of the so-called Oxford Party. Spoke of the heathenism of the poorer classes in London; doubted whether the Saturday half-holiday did not lead to extravagance,

---

[1] Stretton Grandison, where the family home of Homend lies.

inducing men to take excursions, etc, and to use other people's money for that purpose which was entrusted to them for other ends – said it had no effect on the observance of Sunday.

Archdeacon ?Abrahall had his arm broken, and it was so ill set that it became fixed and immoveable; came to London and had it pulled out of its false junction and properly set – 'the most terrible operation', said Ferguson, 'I ever performed'.

Lady Willoughby's church £45,000; the origin of Sidney Herbert's[1] church at Wilton. The old Lady Pembroke had given a party to the Russian Emperor, which cost £1,800, and was found by her clergyman 'advisor' in great self-dissatisfaction, who, to open the way of comfort suggested that as much should be given to the Parish Church as had been bestowed on her fête – which was done; and from that grew up the magnificent church now standing – the bills of which have never been added up, and the cost, therefore, still remains conjectural.

9th October, 1859

Tomorrow, if I live to see it, will end my 39th year. I shall be 40 years old. Never to be better in body, nor, is it likely, in mind, except in that world where human decay and imperfection are unknown, to which God in his good time bring me.

---

[1] Sidney Herbert, 1st Baron Herbert of Lea, Secretary of State for War. His mother (the Dowager Lady Pembroke) was a Russian aristocrat. The church mentioned is that of St Mary and St Nicholas at Wilton in Wiltshire.

How much vanity has been secretly mortified in me – how much still remains. How different in my lot from all that I had anticipated, yet how full of mercy and blessing. How in loneliness is left the best companionship: how in weakness and imperfection may the seeds of perfection be planted. O Lord, fix my mind steadily on my great work, and among all the distractions that lie about me, let me ever remember that I am a Priest of the Altar, and that my work is a spiritual work.

Make me forgiving, Lord, and free from all malice: make me desirous of the salvation of souls, and wise in seeking them.

Fixed last Sunday with Wargen to go and read at his house after church service today – I go and find him gone out, and all empty and silent. O Lord, bring the messages more effectually to him in what way seemeth to thee best. O let no unwise dealing of mine impune thy cause in this place.

10th October, 1859

My birthday. I am 40 years old. 15 years ordained, 4 and 1/2 years at St Weonards, 4 and 1/2 at Lugwardine, 5 and 1/2 years here at Hentland. Oh, how little have I done in all this time – really, solely, and purely for the Love's sake of Jesus Christ. O blessed Lord, whatever thou mayest appoint for me in this world, whether joy or sorrow, life or not life, health or sickness, solitude or companionship, grant that I may more thoroughly feel and know that thou art in me, and I in thee, and that I may be made one by the blessed working of thy Spirit. Make me to live thy Word, to meditate on thee, to seek thy guidance and to escape the snare of slothfulness and walking in the way of old habits. I enter on a new year: O Lord, make it new, in its freedom from sin, in its cheerful activity, its ready benevolence, its kindly feeling, its gentleness and its goodwill to all. Give me power to amend the many sins I have fallen on, and to grow wiser, holier, more uniform in obedience, more weighty and yet more humble every month that I am continued in life.

16th October, 1859

Oh how sadly is this parish sunk in evil, and how impotent have I been to raise it or to cure it. But have I sought it in the pure spirit of humbleness, care and love? I fear not. This week, Joe Wood and his wife quarrelled. He strikes her, drives her out, she supported by her friends in leaving him. He, a Ranter,[1] justifies it 'as in the presence of God', speaking so when not actually sober, and believes in the rightness of his heart, while his life is in more than one point notoriously wicked. Then come blows between Wood and his brother-in-law. Then all the neighbours take up their parts, and our little sink of evil is all in a seething storm. His account of it was highly picturesque, delivered with the energy and intonation of a Ranter, and modulated by a sort of wild grace, which, in spite of his reckless ill-conditioned looks, is a part of the man – 'she reared the murder'.

Then Morgan turns his mother out of his house, where she and son and daughter and young woman just going to be married to the son have been all living in one room. Then Sarah Vaughan, girl of 17 who is mother of a bastard child,

---

[1] 'Ranter' was a term sometimes applied to Primitive Methodists.

comes with no sense of shame, no feeling of impropriety, to stand sponsor to her mother's child, her own brother, while her mother stands sponsor to her base-born boy. This comes on; and Morgan's brother, who, with a wife alive has married another woman. And there are living in the village, at least 4 couples who have not been married: and these are people who are judges of doctrines and particulars in preachers, and sit to hear sermons with a contented satisfaction of look. Surely we have the very foundations to lay, a public opinion to form, to teach people that there is a shame and to bring them to share it. Oh Lord, for wisdom in this matter. Oh grant me patience, perseverance, zeal, faith, honesty, truth, courage, and wisdom to take the right way and follow it up with success, if it seems good to thee, O Lord, from whom all success must come and for whose glory's sake I would endeavour to aim at it, and not for my own credit. Grant this, O Lord, for Jesus Christ's sake, our blessed Lord, our guide and strengthened. Amen.

30th October, 1859

Southey's 'Life of Wesley'[1] – without falsifying he seems to give such a colour to the events which accompanied the use of Methodism, as to leave the impression that we do not see the actual system, but only glimpses of it. The Moravians have the chief share in driving John Wesley to the course he took – driving or leading. The separation from the English church seems to be almost a measure of necessary growth.

---

[1] Robert Southey, *The Life of Wesley, and the Rise and Progress of Methodism*, 1820. He describes many remarkable and dramatic conversion experiences in the early days of Methodism.

The strong love of rule in J Wesley hastened it: but it is hardly possible to conceive a plan, which under the circumstances, could have combined them and the church in one common action. Even now, when the two have approximated in many ways, when clerical attention and watchfulness approaches in many points to the Methodists' plan, and when they have subrided[I] from the exaggeration of their doctrines, the immediate Salvation, the complete assurance, and the perfection: still the history of its earlier stages leaves many doubts as to the possibility of cohesion. The difficulty is not so much in doctrine, or in any definite regulation – even in that of lay preachers, which under the form of lectures might be so organised as to chime in with 'order' – as in the clerical despotism of the Church. The lay element is almost lost; the clergy consider or act as if they considered that in consulting their lay parishioners they were acting ex abundanti gratia[II] – and where lay and cleric differ you generally find the clergyman going his own way, and the layman abiding discontented. I know what the evils of Presbytery have been, and councils of Elders. Lay advisers do have all their evil side, but our faults seem now very much on the other side – stiff in essentials, in smaller points yield to laymen – so, to throw more power into the hands of church wardens would seem to be a useful step in bringing this to a better condition.

Note especially the Lives of the Early Wesley Preachers – J Oliver, Thomas Oliver, Alexander Mather, John Parson, John Haine, Sampson Stainforth, George Storey, Thos Welsh in Ireland.

[I] Subrided: smiled quietly.

[II] ex abundanti gratia: from the abundance of favour, i.e. from the goodness of their hearts.

20th November, 1859

A wandering month – or at least two weeks away. To Homend for Rent day, then with Fanny and her children to Weymouth via Chippenham, Yeovil etc and back after one day's stay. The circle of buildings which surrounds the bay is no doubt fine, and the bay itself is open and extensive, and the outline of the hills is prettily diversified on each side, but with all these favourable points the whole result is uninteresting and poor. The Chesil Bank is a real curiosity, though the gradual diminution of the size of the stone is, I should say, mythical, or at least has been exaggerated.

Met Bevan and Grove: the last a rather noticeable man. He is self-educated, and occupies the position of Secretary of the Crystal Palace Company, in addition to which he is sub-editor of Murray's Biblical Encyclopaedia. His Palace duties occupy him from 10 till 6, and he works at his Biblical matters till 2. But this is not likely to last long, as no constitution can stand such wear, and already he complains of nervous pains, etc. We walked to the Chesil Bank; he was well read, in Old English divinity especially, but did not seem to have a very large grasp, or much poetry of feeling. He 'carried through the prep' as the phrase is.

Stanley, Sinai and Palestine.[1] It was rather amusing to hear how the little literary affair in which the two gentlemen were engaged seemed in their eyes to convert them into literary men, who could settle the world of authors and publishers by

---

[1] *Sinai and Palestine*, written by Arthur Stanley, biblical historian, and published in 1856.

their 'ipsi dixerunt'.[1] Bevan, too, is overworked, and taking a long rest from parish (Hay), pupils, and not from writing.

To Cheltenham to buy furniture for the curatage. Lunch with the Parkinsons, and so to London. Biddulph – Leddon – British Museum. On my way there to see a certain book, the life of Richard Lyle, when I turned into Russell Smith's[II] to pay a bill; which over, I asked if he had anything relating to Herefordshire. He said one book, which I never had in my possession before – the Life of Mr Lyle, and there was my object of search.

To Battersea, where dined with Clark-Mitchell, School Inspector; Capt Claxton-James, etc, etc, etc. Mitchell's arbitrary notions and contempt of local education authorities were rather noticeable – curious accounts of Beller.

His nature Higgins followed his mother's – 'for beauty and for glory' – travelled, after disappearing from the university, with a show; an old lady was taken by the excellence of his delivery, and was the means of his taking orders. Visit to Macready who examined him and listened and finally said – 'Sir, you will never do for the stage – perhaps you may for the pulpit'.

Claxton said he had made a fourth with Hook, Matthews and another, and seen them drink 4 bottles of brandy after supper, while their cabs were waiting.

---

[1] 'they have themselves said'.
[II] In Soho Square, London.

27th November, 1859

Pride finds an entrance at any cranny, and, once in, spreads like the famous 'genius', till it becomes 'an awful figure of 50 feet high'. It is fed on humility, and fed on praise: it feeds in society, and pastures in solitude. Idleness pampers it, and study strengthens it. Poetry gives it wings, and drier subjects, history, even divinity find it wheels to move with. Active dealing with men gives it a thousand little points on which it settles, to which it clings, and the mere holding aloof and gliding through life, without actual interchange of dealing with others leaves room for that ideal picturing of possibilities, which is not the worst school of this apt scholar. Then it combines, so skilfully with other feelings, which seem remote enough in their nature from it that it leads to others, and grows out of others with which no connection could have been anticipated. Good nature, kindness, liberality, all these might, perhaps, be not unnaturally the avenues of its approach – but that it should grow out of failure – out of ordinary duties which could not without shame be omitted, out of things, altogether beyond a man's will, is a strange evidence of its intrusiveness. It was said that pride and vanity were by nature contrary: and yet experience shows them co-existent in the same individual. If there are people whose good word may flatter, Vanity leads to aim at this gratification. If there are none, then Pride supplies the place, and constructs the praise which was not given. Oh, if instead of praise, blame, opposition, even ridicule are distributed, 'at mihi plaudo ipse domi'[1] – and the ignorance, misjudgement, imperfect appreciation or unpenetrating intelligence of others furnish very comforting meditations after all.

---

[1] 'but I cheer myself when in my own house'.

O man, thou child of dust, tossing without will of thine upon the ocean of the world, thy place of birth, thy name, thy station, thy shape and temperament, thy companions and tastes, all in great part without choice of thine bestowed on thee – wilt thou still nourish high thoughts, and flatter thyself with vain dreams, ever excusing thy failures by some plausible cloke; and taking to thy own especial credit, the successes that fall in thy way. Be wiser than so: and find thy wisdom in folly, thy greatness in a lowly mind, thy pride in humility. Lift up thine eyes to the hills, where on the throne of real glory stands the Rebuker of all Pride, who walked in meekness through the world, and now from on high sends thee power to tend thy swelling heart, and to subdue the stirrings of this corrupt feeling within thee ... [*followed by prayer.*]

Christmas Day, 1859

After strange vicissitudes of weather, Christmas chose for its appearance at last a dull, cold, half frozen mist, which drew up about 1 o'clock and fell again at four in steady determined rain. Ice was collected in October, fair and mild weather followed in November, December opened with frost, which at one period carried the thermometer down to 28 degrees, below freezing point. Then came mild rain, then frost again, and thus we have passed the turning point of the year and move on towards a new date. During this time I have been almost continuously struggling to overtake time, as usual without much success, but finding fresh proof of the truth of the old adage: 'Lose an hour in the morning and look for it all the day.'

I have indeed spent a good deal of time in going backwards and forwards to Homend, where I am having my picture taken, as so only could I get my mother to sit for hers. A clever young artist by name Mon is staying there for the purpose. Something creditable about him. His father, an auctioneer in York, left him the eldest of ten children, and not more than 20 years old. These he has brought up, and pushed on till they are now in a fair way to earn a livelihood, and to do this he regrets that he has had to exchange 'high art' for portraits, fame for money, and been compelled to paint for the pot. But as he is now but 28 there is a possibility of striking out into the more shining waters. I should think he had been thrown into some doubt as to his religious opinions, though now, I hear from Ian Heywood, that he is settled. But he told me that he had been staying with a man of talent and scientific attainment, who was known in the literary world (was it Dr Henry?), who said 'I believe in God the Father Almighty, maker of heaven and earth, and of all things visible and invisible, and there I stop' – and he went on to state that 5 out of the 6 scientific men with whom he associated at the Athenaeum and elsewhere had really the same abbreviated faith, – esoteric however, as they passed before the world as Christians. This man said, 'I go to church because of my wife and daughters, for I wish them to be Christians'. And when I said that this was detestable and mischievous hypocrisy, blinding the eyes of Christians, and originating probably as much in regard to self, and to the loss which an open denial of the Christian doctrine would entail in worldly consideration, I thought that my auditor winced. His deist said that Christianity was the most beautiful of the visions of belief which had passed over the world: others had been beautiful and they had died away – and this too would

pass after them. Alas! For the individual mind to weigh
and balance evidence, if no difference can be seen in any
strength and weight of evidence between the Gospel and its
predecessors or would-be rivals.

To Dewchurch – Advent lecture, ditto All Saints Hereford; a
larger congregation at the country parish than in the town.

Poor old Betty Pymble died on Monday, after two years of
confinement to bed – with a cheerful contentment and a
humble and patient expectation of a better lot which ripened
towards her tranquil end. Blind and helpless, and ignorant
and friendless, and without those rapturous expectations
by which some are supported, she yet showed such a steady
scriptural trust, though without assurance, that it will rest as
a pleasant spot in my memory.

Poor Powell has been struck with apoplexy, and remains
now for a week in a state of insensibility; a worthy, honest
man, who raised himself from the condition of a labourer
to the occupation of a small farm. Watkins' wife, at New
Inn, lies dangerously ill, in a most becoming and acquiescent
state of mind, though three small children and a kind
husband might seem to make the possibility of parting
bitter in her eyes. Thus the uncertainties of life are before
our eyes, and here they seem to fall on those who, few and
widely scattered, are the salt of our society. Lord, fill their
places, and though it is humiliating, I think how little part
I have had in establishing, building up, or ripening these
Christians against their trial, yet they show me that it is not
in the hearts and minds of these people that the incapacity
for reception of God's spirit rests; and if I have his help, and

labour wisely, constantly, spiritually – there may arise light
in the darkness, fresh souls may be added to the company of
the Saints, and the light of new examples may shine among
us. [*Followed by prayer.*]

Mr James, schoolmaster, has left after 5 years – a curious
mixture of efficiency and neglect, who has, however, I fear,
left no moral impression behind him, and I fear that it may be
owing in part to my neglect in not pointing out to him with
frequency and plainness the faults and failings which I saw.

1st January, 1860

In the midst of sweeping winds and darkness, wet with
rain, the old year sank into the gulf of emptiness; and with
the roar of the south-west wind and gusty driven storms,
the New Year took its seat upon the throne of the present.
Who can foresee what shall befall before it too shall sink
down and be gone. There is ... in the world: one man holds
in his hand, not indeed the destinies of the world, but its
direction through those calmer periods, when the real spirit
of great nations is only half awake. If England, or Prussia, or
Russia had fixed and firm resolves and purposes which were
national, they would doubtless guide and bend the political
views of Napoleon.[1] But while they are distracted, he is on
the watch. While they avoid commotion, he rather seeks it:
while they have the peace and prosperity of their subjects
to regard, he has his own security to fix, and this depends

---

[1] Napoleon III was the first President of France from 1848 to 1852 and the
Emperor of the French from 1852 to 1870. A nephew of Napoleon Bonaparte, he
was the last monarch to rule over France.

on his feeding the vanity of the French people and finding employment for their touchy and fight loving army. And how many questions are hung on to this disposition of events? The Pope and his government, the Italian independence, Austria and her provinces, Turkey and Egypt, India and China. Nothing hardly that through the wide world comes within the thousand 'feelers' of civilisation can altogether withdraw itself from the consideration of Louis Napoleon and his hidden intents. Such is the power of unity, of a single mind ruling over a great nation, and disposing at his will of its immense material force; yet the weakness of it too! An illness – an 'accident' – a shot – and the whole becomes the 'baseless fabric of a dream', and the French nation is again that maelstrom of ten thousand currents which we have more than once seen.

England, feeling the reaction from the Reign of Cotton,[I] is forming itself into Rifle companies[II] from one end of the land to the other: a confession that there is something in national life more noble than money, more precious than luxury. The Whigs have so filled the offices, and saturated the papers and journals with their appointments, that a ministry professing little more than the late Conservative government goes quietly on – while that had 10,000 open mouths finding holes and inserting fables and poisoning minds, that the share of

---

[I] 'King Cotton': massive import of raw cotton to Britain prior to the American Civil War, on which one sixth of the population of Britain was dependent for their livelihoods. As a result of the war, mills closed, workers lost their jobs, and England's cotton manufacturing districts in the counties of Lancashire and Cheshire experienced widespread poverty.

[II] It was at this time that in response to growing tensions between Britain and France, many counties promoted the formation of volunteer Rifle Corps, which were the forerunners of our present Territorial Army.

loaves and fishes might fall to the young Whigs and not to the Conservative striplings. Eheu! – both alike have yet to find that higher aim.

The Parsonage is covered in, and if unreasonable delay should not occur, will be finished in the Spring. O Lord, send thy blessing on it, and on those who shall from generation to generation inhabit it; that they who own it may make it their chief work to spread the knowledge of thee and thy ways in the people of the parish committed to them, and that true religion and piety may flourish and abound the more from its being built here. If I am allowed to inhabit it, make me more wise and diligent, active and self-denying, bold and loving than I have hitherto been – and grant that if it seems good to thee, the way may be opened to a Christian plan of living, and to a wise exchange of hospitality with my neighbours; and grant that, if it be after thy will, and if it seems best in thy wisdom, that there may be added the crown of a man's days – a Christian and amiable wife. But this as thou wilt, and not as I in my ignorance fancy to be best. Make me for the years to come more active and wise, systematic and regular, patient and earnest. Enable me to cure my especial fault – late rising, neglect of study of scripture, close hearty conversation with my parishioners – and those more personal sins which I have from time to time note.

Oh Lord, enable me to put away these all, that I may by thy help grow in grace, and become more fit and ready to obey thy call whenever it shall come – at evening or at midnight or at cockcrow, that thou mayest find me watching. Blessed is that servant whom his Lord, when he cometh shall find so doing. Amen.

This is the first mention that Poole makes in the diary of his new parsonage, so long in the building at Kynaston. He hasn't given up hope of getting married, either.

8th January, 1860

Tennyson says of a painter painting a portrait, that under the
face 'the shape and colour of a mind and life', he finds the man.[1]

In early years fair nature forms the face a fresco-tablet,
    mouldable and soft,
Where every breath of heaven may write its mark.
But long ere three score years have bowed the back,
That little innocent dimple-mottled thing
Becomes a disk, self-registered, to show
What, in the living foundry of the brain
Has been received, retained or reproduced,
To what transmuted, by what purpose shaped
The bubbling passionate tempers of the child.

and idle words go floating round the world
till back they come, armed with the biting steel,
to print their record on the parent lips.

---

[1] Alfred Lord Tennyson had his portrait painted by George Frederick Watts in 1857, and is said to have questioned the artist about his thoughts when painting, and then developed the answer into poetry.

29th January, 1860

Parliament has met, quietly and rather dully. But things seem to point at a serious struggle for the church. A small and active body are fixed to disestablish it, and though the large majority are inclined to support it, yet the old case recurs, partly from indolence, partly from political motives, partly with a mistaken notion of disarming opposition and satisfying opponents; the friends of the church yield point after point, and when at last they find the error – that every concession is used as a standing place for fresh attack – it may be too late to remedy. God keep us from this trial, and make us clergy to see that something more than indolent respectability and gentlemanly negligence are needed, if the Church of England is to hold its place as the National Church of the land.

I admire in common with all my countrymen the splendid talents of Mr Gladstone,[I] and the elegance which sets them off: I am proud of him as a member of my university, and I have the most undoubting faith in the honesty both of his public and private life. But I fear that in church matters, he is playing the part of Lord Falkland,[II] so sadly expiated on the field of Newberry: a part which once played should be for the teaching of ages, which is summed up in three short words: to hesitate, to palliate, to regret.

[I] William Ewart Gladstone, Chancellor of the Exchequer at this time, then later Tory then Liberal Prime Minister of the UK.

[II] Lucius Carey, 2nd Viscount Falkland, killed at the Battle of Newbury in 1643. Attributed to Falkland is the dictum, 'When it is not necessary to make a decision, it is necessary not to make a decision'.

5th February, 1860

Parliament has met: the Pope and Napoleon have come to a rupture.[I] Italy is gathering up its forces, and Venice, still under Austrian rule, and fretting indignantly at its master, promises to be the detonating powder that shall explode the whole. A 'cohere' lies for the contemplation of the world in this coming spring.

To come from the wide history of the world to my own corner, a meeting of clergymen and Christianity of Archenfield Deanery was held on Friday to defend church rates. About 40 assembled, the first ...... ever held in this deanery, at least since the Reformation, whatever may have been the case before, or however the old kings of 'Ergyng'[II] may have consulted with their Lords 'Spiritual' as well as temporal.

If old Bishop Swinfield[III] could survey the assembled clergy, would he have found the change for the better or for the worse? Probably in the whole deanery there would have been several religious houses: Monkton, Kilpeck, Holme Lacy, and during the Templars' days, Garway and Harewood. Some better artists, painters, glass stainers, manuscript writers, he might have found, but as an average assembly of respectables, we might fairly challenge the old Bishop to the comparison.

[I] For many centuries up to 1859, most of what is now Italy was under the direct sovereign rule of the Pope, as the Papal States. However, by 1861, much of the Papal States' territory had been conquered and incorporated into the Kingdom of Italy. Initially, Napoleon III of France supported the Pope in resisting this takeover, but later had to withdraw his support.

[II] Ergyng was the Welsh name for the kingdom of Archenfield.

[III] Richard Swinfield, Bishop of Hereford 1282–1317.

Number of resident seculars in Archenfield in 13th century?
Swinfield only visited in 1289, Monmouth, Llanwarne and
Kilpeck, passing through St Weonards (only a chapelry of
Lugwardine), and Much Dewchurch, without notice. Tretire
lay near his round, and Welsh Newton actually upon it, and
Bridstow and Peterstow little off it, but none of them were 'on
his list'. Why was this?

19th February, 1860

We draw near Lent. May I have the wisdom to make good
use of it, and restore, if it may be, the things that are decayed
by sloth, vanity or worldly feeling. Read J Taylour (or some
equivalent book) and put together the bones of Reformation
history by reading Burnett's 'Abridgement', not scorning on
this matter the advice even of Lord Chesterfield. Less than
this, I must not be content with, though I must remember
that Parsonage house building is a very engrossing work and
has stolen many an hour from Parish and from Study, and
will still rob many more from the various avocations of my
life, before I can say there is a Parsonage for the 'Gospellers'
of Hentland for generations yet to come.

26th February, 1860

St Yves was a Breton saint who lived in the latter half of
the 13th century, dying in 1303, at the age of 50. He seems
to have been a good parish priest, and was 'official' to two
bishops. He was remarkable, in his legal position, for his
efforts to bring about amicable arrangements, and for himself

undertaking the defence of the poorer people who appeared in the Bishop's Court. He refused to profit by his share of fees, which he gave to the poor. In his clerical life, he had two parishes, one for 10 years and the other for 8, giving up one when he was appointed to the second. There he was a 'painful' preacher,[1] not only in his own parish but in other churches in the neighbourhood, and in all his journeys he was accustomed to go on foot, 'though he could well afford a good horse.' It was noted as a sign of his excellence in the pulpit that people who had heard him preach in the morning would follow him to a distant church to listen to him again. Kindness and persuasion were the mark of his style.

In his private life he was liberal and austere, giving away in alms the whole proceeds of his cure, and observing the fasts with such rigour, that through Lent and Advent he lived wholly on bread and water, as he did also on other fast days in the year. Nor was his indulgence in sleep more free than in food, as he lay on a hard couch with a book or a stone by way of pillows, and seldom 'except when worn out by work' slept through the whole night. How his name came to be transferred to the county of Huntingdon does not appear.

4th March, 1860

From numerous sources comes the complaint that the 'higher minds' – the more honest and enthusiastic, are turning their steps to any other channel of duty rather than to the ministry of the Church. In the last ten years the diminution in the

---

[1] A painful preacher: he 'took pains' to preach earnestly.

numbers at Oxford who have entered into Holy Orders is stated to be very striking, and many reasons are thrown out to account for it: the growth of unbelief, says Vaughan,[I] with the example of those shipwrecks of the faith, which the last few years have exhibited; the intolerance of commonplace orthodoxy, says Stanley,[II] which confines all speculation to a narrowly grooved line, and would regard as heretic, and treat as criminal any who overstep this (which he says in especial allusion to Jowett).[III]

To these reasons may be added the very rapid growth of fortunes in the last few years which has a double effect. It induces parents to guide their sons into some of those avenues of livelihood which 'pay' better than Holy Orders, and so withdraws a large element of former clergy; and it induces a large number who have made a fortune above their social status to put their sons into Orders – who bring there what are called 'low connections' – un-gentlemanlike associations and habits, and are by degrees giving a lower tone of feeling, and repelling the higher classes, the refined, the exclusive.

I remember when it was spoken of as a great joke and marvel that Griffiths, who kept the Angel at Oxford, talked of his son taking orders, and Fig the tailor at Oxford was rather a marked man because his boy was at Rugby and went on to Ordination. Now the instances are numerous enough to make us marvel at the marvelling.

[I] Charles Vaughan, headmaster of Harrow.
[II] Arthur Stanley, dean of Westminster.
[III] Benjamin Jowett, master of Balliol College.

Then the subdivision of Parishes and the formation of Peel
Districts have altered the condition of the Church. There are
few or none of those little Bishoprics, where, under the guise
of a parish priest, a man might enjoy an Episcopal fortune,
and exercise hardly less than a bishop's influence, with all
the ease and comfort of private life. And the numerous new
churches with a bare endowment of £100–150 per annum,
with a population of the lower middle class – touchy and
ill-mannered, requiring much attention, yet not knowing how
to receive it, repel a clergyman of refinement or fortune, and
oppress one who is poor, except he be of that rough and hard
nature which is drawn from the ranks of his parishioners and
assimilates with them.

Moreover, the conduct of nearly every party in the Church
seems to have its share in augmenting the dislike of the
better class of mind to ordination. The 'high church' as
they are called with their rubrical operations, their affected
singularity of dress and speech and manners, their short-
sighted insistence on some infinitely small point of ceremony
which they dignify into the name of a principle, have roused
a disgraceful outcry against their party, and have caused a
blow to the fine independence and action of the Church,
and subjected it, by more than one example, to an unknown
pressure of popular opinion, and would make one of clear
independent belief hesitate before he entered on a state which
might bring him into such collision.

The 'low church' – evangelical, as they are called, have no
less to answer for. To their violent denunciation of all that
differed from themselves we owe many a feeling of disgust at
Religion itself, of which they proclaim themselves the especial

champions and last home. Their vulgar ways, their narrow views, their limited conception, their stereotyped prayers – all would rather drive back than invite an open, honest high-minded man, who wished to walk in a straightforward path by the light of Scripture and the rule of the English church. The 'high and dry', the 'dreary and dull', the 'slack and sleepy', the 'sporting and spoony':[1] all in their degree; but not more, perhaps, than of old, are notices against entering.

The number of desertions to Rome has doubtless had some effect, giving the notion of a dishonesty and instability, which a clever, rather truth-seeking man might fear that he might, by long study and closer insight, be led into himself. And the distribution of Patronage also aids – 'You know his connection with us is very much against him', said Lady Hardwicke last year of Canon Jukes' promotion to Bangor – when Lord Hardwicke was first Lord of the Admiralty under Lord Derby.

And one more reason only: the requirements of a modern parish life. The begging and school teaching, and speaking and visiting – so much more than in ancient days – breaks in very seriously and fatally on a regular course of study. Men who are by nature and inclination desirous of a life of deep systematic study would be more likely to seek it in a purely literary life, than in that which was the literary life of a past generation. The ease of a comely Parsonage and the library of theological authors – and this tends to depreciate the study of scientific theology, as the clerical profession guided the line of reading, and connected it with the main duty of life. But

---

[1] Spoony: over-sentimental.

without this link to theological studies, it will depend on a thousand varying influences down which many of the streams of knowledge a man may choose to float.

The practical question is how to prevent this tendency from becoming injurious to the interests of the Church: how to check it, if it is already so far advanced; how to win back to the ranks of the clergy those in the rising generation who, in talent and character and station, high feeling, noble purpose and truthful impulses, are the most valuable aiders, necessary indeed, to the great coming struggle.

18th March, 1860

Every month shows more strikingly the altered position of ecclesiastical affairs, and the disposition which exists in the House of Commons to deal with them in an innovating and rather hostile manner. It is not so many years back that matters connected with the church were of rare occurrence, of slender interest, and of debateless formality in the business of the House. But session by session we have seen questions leaping into importance, which are of essential consequence to the welfare and position of the Church, and we have seen them dealt with in a spirit of increasing Puritanism and hostility, if not to the Church, yet at least to the present rules and government of the Church. It is of no weight that the words of all are full of professed regard to the success of the national Church, and to the spread of real religion in the country; for when the point is tried, we find that it must be real religion after some special views, a gospel according to the Hon. Member for Poole, and a church guided, governed and remodelled after the idiosyncrasies of some crotchety orator. And as the indifference of former years passes away, and they who have been brought up during the ferment of Oxford disputes come into the more prominent portions of public life, we must look for fixed and strong opinion on church and religion. So my old friend Danby Seymour,[1] by no means a bad or mischievous man, conscientious, considerate, careful and painstaking, is the one to legislate on clergymen's dress, and to denounce with some bitterness of spirit the autocratic authority of the Parochial clergyman.

1) Compare the proceedings in Parliament from James Ist to the Rebellion: and the gradually increasing proportion of church debates, of matters connected with religion, with the course of things during the last 10 or 15 years – and there will be found, I think, a very instructive resemblance.

2) Count the acts of Parliament and their effects which have modified and changed the position of the Established Church since its settlement at the Reformation. It will be found, I think, that the whole tendency of legislation has been to tie the Church more completely to the State; while scarcely in any case has enlarged freedom of action or increased adaptability to changed circumstances been the result of the proceedings. So that the Church at this day, while more than ever checked and controlled by the state, and less able to follow its own views of what is needful and just, is altogether in different relations to the State from what it was at first, after the Reformation.

---

[1] Henry Danby Seymour, Liberal MP for Poole from 1850 to 1868.

The State seems to need a slave tied to it, whom it can whip and ill-treat at pleasure, but whose remonstrance must be treated as rebellion; whose dime after a free ride is ingratitude and folly.

25th March, 1860. Lady Day.

Glimpses of light appear narrow openings in the clouds which whirl onwards under the roaring March winds, and show that there is a bright, calm background above these shades and turmoil. Ah, and in the daily sight of that sunny core, breathing its soft air and inhaling its rich sunlight I might, but for my own fault, be now living. Each touch of that better, purer, gentler air brings with it the half-whispered reproach. Why not more? Why not constantly? Ah, why indeed. The beckoning voices are not wanting – the sympathetic taste is, perhaps, existing; those aspirations spread out the folds of their rich draperies and shed aromatic dews upon the dreamer's head. And yet the hard, coarse, unmellowed outline of the rough world, without a recommendation to support it, or an excuse to encourage it, can be drawn in effacing colours over the more precious work. Never schoolman or monk effaced a more precious treasure for the record of his service book or the Summa Theologica.[1]

---

[1] The *Summa Theologica*, as its title indicates, is a 'theological summary'. It seeks to describe the relationship between God and man and to explain how man's reconciliation with the Divine is made possible at all through Christ.

Oh Lord, give me grace to follow thy leading: to remove all
obstacles – to stand before thee, to walk with thee, to be led
by thee: that I might be thine for ever. Per JC, Amen

*It sounds as if Poole may have been offered a post abroad, in sunnier climes, which
he has rejected.*

8th April, Easter Day, 1860

Again I have been allowed to keep our Easter Festival, to
meet my brethren in God's house, and share with them
the bread and the wine, in sure proof of the Resurrection.
[*Followed by prayer.*]

8th July, 1860. Cam.

A holiday of 3 Sundays leaves me, the first time for many a
day, to find this a real Sabbath, and in the glory of a summer
sun, whose heat is snatched away by the fresh north wind,
and in the fresh beauty of this various and fruitful county I
can enjoy it to perfection, nooked in under the shelter of the
broken Cotswold hills, just where they overlook the rich vale
of Berkely, with Stinchcombe lifting its green shaven crown
out of its beech tree circle, and wrapping it round on one side,
while the Cam Peak and Longdown border it on the other,
and while the end is lost among the mazes and intricacies
of Uley Barrow and the Ridge. The Vale of Cam with its
2 churches lies along – a very haven of sensuous beauty:
one open side stretches away up the Severn where ridges of
tree-covered banks cross the plain, one behind another in

the gradations of soft blue distance, till the old Tower of
Gloucester writes its more distinct outlines on the horizon.
The valley itself is strewn with the cheerful stone houses, set
thick among the elms, and a clear stream bubbles along the
bottom, keeping a constant companionship to the railway
that runs by its side, and with no ambitious embankments,
or formidable cuttings, gives the picture all the addition of
thoughts of energy and life, without defacing in a single spot
the rural completeness of landscape. To Stinchcombe, where
Sir George Prevost[I] lives the life of a parish priest; Isaac
Williams[II] also lives in the parish, helping in the services
according as his feeling of health and strength permit. He is a
striking picture: his pale and rather florid cast of feature, with
grey hair and well-marked, prominent nose – the dark and
life-full eye, and the thinness both of feature and body which
makes him look like one shrinking up into himself with pain;
though the calmness and gentle smoothness of his manner
correct the earlier notion. He rode with us as we walked on
the hills, and he entered heartily into the points of the view,
deploring the mist which hung over the distance, 'worse than
he had seen during the whole winter'. He wears a black cap
on his head, in service and out, a striking addition to the look
of the man.

In the early nineteenth century, different groups vied for power and influence
within the Church of England. Many, particularly in high office, saw themselves
as Latitudinarian (liberal). Conversely, many clergy in the parishes were

---

[I] Sir George Prevost, baronet, perpetual curate of Stinchcombe; archdeacon of
Gloucester from 1865 to 1881, and honorary canon of Gloucester Cathedral from
1859 until his death. Prominent Tractarian.

[II] Isaac Williams, brother-in-law to Prevost. Also a prominent Tractarian, and able
leader of the Oxford Movement.

Evangelicals, as a result of the revival led by John Wesley. Alongside these, the universities, particularly Oxford, began to develop a movement to restore liturgical and devotional customs which borrowed heavily from Roman Catholicism, before and after the Reformation: this group became known as the Oxford Movement.

In Oxford, the movement was centred in Oriel College, where Poole was later a student. It eventually developed into Anglo-Catholicism. The movement's philosophy was known as Tractarianism after its series of publications, the Tracts for the Times, published from 1833 to 1841.

The Oxford Movement resulted in the establishment of Anglican religious orders, both of men and of women. It incorporated ideas and practices which incorporated more powerful emotional symbolism in the church. Its effects were so widespread that the Eucharist gradually became more central to worship, vestments became common, and numerous Roman Catholic practices were re-introduced into worship, and this continues to be the case up to the present time.

Partly because bishops often refused to give livings to Tractarian priests, many of them began working in slums. From their new ministries, they developed a critique of British social policy, both local and national, taking an interest in issues such as the just wage, the system of property renting, infant mortality and industrial conditions.

A number of priests who were influenced by the Oxford Movement were eventually received into the Roman Catholic Church.

Judging by Poole's interest in Prevost and Williams in the last diary entry, this is where his sympathies lay, and this would certainly fit in with the symbolism and ornateness of Hoarwithy Church.

9th August, 1860

From July 5th till this day, I have been a wanderer perforce – not always away, but never in a house of my own.

From Power to Lea's at Droitwich, thence to Hereford and Homend, and so on to Penpont to see Perry Williams and back on Saturday – to service – the next week finding my house all unfinished; after, lodging at Pengethly [sic] – to Phillerts – Bowmeeting – Homend. Pengethly again for Sunday: to Perrystone, the George Clive's,[I] where great friendliness, altogether undeserved, and now at last, 'post tot discrimina rerum',[II] to sleep in the New Parsonage at Hentland. It was begun in July last year, and tho' not yet finished, is yet sufficiently advanced to lodge me and Mrs Townsend, my new housekeeper. I had one of those many unrecorded presentiments, (for those that fail are seldom mentioned,) that I should never live to occupy the house that I was building. But by God's mercy, I have been suffered to come thus far. May he bless it to the parish and to me, and to all those who, in long succession, may hereafter occupy it, as ministers of this parish. [*Followed by prayer.*]

One thing seems now more than ever needed for my comfort. But God is wiser than we are, and if it may be offered to me, I would at once accept it. I set this before me to follow it with, I hope, a wise and sound purpose, being sure that it will contribute, in all sobriety of human judgement at least, to my usefulness, happiness and moral good. The loneliness strikes very chill; the voiceless evening, the un-goodnighted retirement, the turn from book to bed. No lightening of human intercourse intervening is depressing to the feelings, and, I feel sure, bad for the intellectual, sanitary and moral condition. [*Followed by prayer.*]

[I] George Clive, Member of Parliament and barrister, of Perrystone Court, Herefordshire.

[II] 'after so many various circumstances'.

26th August – 17th October, 1860

All this time I have lived a temporary, unsettled life –
being in my new home, indeed, but only in an upstairs
room: unfurnished above, and unfinished below: which
unsettlement is the more complete as I have been continually
from week to week promised the completion of the work, and
continually till this day been disappointed by the delays and
errors of the tradesmen.

It is a little mortifying to find how one's mental condition, the
order and method of thought, the systematic arrangement
of time, and the unembarrassed fulfilment of routine duties,
are all upheaved or depressed, brought to fault by this
mode of living. But 'man is man and master of his lot', says
Tennyson, and, no doubt, in emergent circumstances, under
excitement or at the call of great duties, these little outward
embarrassments would be burst like Sampson's bonds.
But their continual presence, and under every variety of
feeling, their steady unvaried pressure, never yielding, never
departing, overpower the ordinary resolutions of men of
common determination of character. So, I have seen families
of some talents, with better notions of things than the greater
part of those about them, come into a neighbourhood,
resolved to take a lead, to alter things and give a tone of the
fashions of society, and after a little, the power of common
ordinary minds, less able in every point than theirs, has, by
dull resistance and instructive continuance in accustomed
habits proved too strong for the proposed innovations,
and the clever, lively family has been compelled to follow
in the old track, its only consolation and sign of inferiority
consisting in a hearty grumble at the stupidity of the world.

A confirmation has taken place, which absence and this life has, I fear, prevented me from making as useful as it should have been made.

And my birthday has again passed by. [*Followed by prayer.*]

3rd November, 1860

The house is pronounced done – complete in all essentials, and may be forthwith fitted up; a great relief to the mind.

'Good angels watch around our home
And we are one day nearer thee
Through life's long day and death's dark night
O gentle Jesus be our light.'

But even his new house fails to cheer William up.

28th February, 1861

Three months, since I last wrote record: three months of bitter, wintry weather without, and of disarrangement and unsettledness within, with a long, lonely Christmas, which penetrated the new house and chilled me in feeling and thought. At Christmas, my cousin Lydia Graves died, a sudden and unexpected death. My mother and sisters have been, at different times, seeing me in my Parsonage, and the parish work has moved on with too listless and unhopeful step. And thus, while heaven and earth are coming together, while the 'still, deep music of humanity' is sounding its solemn diapasons on all sides, I record in cold, thankless, unemphatic commonplace the events of three months of life. Three months of 90 days, 90 days of 24 hours each – of those hours so limited to us all – so sure to be recalled with regret, if wasted in dreamy indolence or regretful idealisms. No, let a wiser and higher line of duty guide me continually. What I am, I have in great measure made myself: the hindrances and follies which have stood in my way have been the natural offshoots of what I did not cope with early enough, not at all with sufficient manliness.

There is a strength yet which should forbid despair. There is a vigour, which will not be refused, if it be heartily aimed at, encouraged, fostered, and wisely drawn out. What is so mean – so worldly – so contrary to the 'assurance of a man' is this shilly-shally, up and down, backwards and forward course.

10th March, 1861

Sunday morning. My new abode, and my not having a school as yet ordered, allow me leisure on a Sunday morning to mark the seaboard of life, instead of making it the last work of the evening. Oh why should the monotony of this life – the absence of conversation – be so wearing to me? Surely I am not so gifted in the art of Society as to claim as my due any especial attention, and yet there are subjects on which I fain would talk: there are thoughts which would out, and impressions which others could quicken and correct, and these, it seems to me, are somewhat choked by absence of opportunity. But if this self living thought is fallen to me 'in the way of business,' as old Turnbull says, shall I not make it the very thing of all others most profitable and expedient – and if I complain of this, now that it is about me, should I not as certainly be discontented with whatever other variety of life might be assigned to me. Every spray on which a life can be hung has its thorn budding; some, it may be, are more unpleasantly placed, in some innocuously protuberant, but why not hide the point in that unpierceable covering which is within the power of all to obtain. If pride and vanity were utterly mortified – as they are not – if perfect acquiescence in the will of the Life director were cheerfully accepted – all these thoughts would take wings. And there would spring up in the actual performance of duty in the commonplaces of life, that inward interest which can tide them over the 'cheery intercourse of daily life,' and land them in the happiness which springs from a common communication with those higher powers by which our life is surrounded, ennobled, and inspirited.

Easter Day, 1861

Two full congregations, a rare sight here! 30 communicants at Hentland.

The deaths or incapacity of Poole's father and older brothers left him, the youngest son, with responsibilities to the family estates, and the necessity of travelling back to Stretton Grandison to keep an eye on things there.

7th April, 1861

Communion at Little Dewchurch. A week of absence in the mixed vocation of business and pleasure: at Homend, to meet agent. Diocesan board. Proprietary school, and to Stoke. There were Duke and Duchess of Montrose, Lady Violet and Lord Ronald Graham, Lord Llanover,[I] Lady Anna and Katrina Loftus etc. One morning, I was the sole untitled one among the party, and it would astonish some of the denouncers of aristocracy to see the complete unpretending simplicity of their ways. I have seen infinitely more assumption in country clergymen, exalted above their fellows by having written a book, or preached some public sermon. Lord Llanover told much of Garibaldi,[II] whom he had been with at Naples. He described him as being a 'child in politics', easily deceived; made himself to be the suggester of some of his mores: the secularisation of marriage, and the abolition of internal passports, he notably attributed to himself. Said he was with the deputation when on their road to meet Garibaldi: they were met by the announcement of his immediate arrival, and if he had not suggested that they should send people on to prepare the city, to tell the route and to get up an excitement, he said 'the thing would have been a failure'. While they were looking each other in the face, he suggested this course, and suddenly the leader of the company flung his arms round his neck in gratitude.

[I] Lord Lieutenant of Monmouthshire at this time.

[II] Giuseppe Garibaldi: Italian general, patriot, revolutionary and republican. He contributed to Italian unification and the creation of the Kingdom of Italy.

All Naples was unhinged from its propriety. He saw women of the town embracing respectable priests, and bundled together in the same carriage, and he himself, walking along the town, was overtaken by a carriage containing 2 gentlemen and 2 ladies, evidently of the upper classes. As they passed him, they saw he was English, and cried 'Viva Inghilterra'. He replied 'Viva la bellezza d'Italia'. Suddenly one of the men jumped out, handed him in, and got up upon the box himself, and thus he drove about during half the day with ladies whom he never saw before or after.

The upper orders of the clergy are against the new state of things,[I] but the lower ones go with it, and are gainers by it, as a large portion of the monastic revenues are appropriated to the parish clergy. But his extreme wrath and ill word were devolved to the Pope and those around him. But as he (Llanover) was only a short time at Rome, his stories would be secondhand; yet the mother-in-law of Burn? ought to have some foundation for saying that the Pope had been on too intimate terms with an Englishman's widow, the same that went off with him to Gaeta[II] in 1848.

The 7th April was the date of the 1861 Census. It records Poole's household, containing himself, as the perpetual curate of Hentland, and his three servants: Jane White, 34, who came from Shaftesbury, and Isabella Phillips, 21, from Gloucester, both general servants, and George Hughes from Chester, aged 20, the groom.

[I] i.e. the conquest of the Papal States by the Kingdom of Italy.

[II] In 1848, Pope Pius IX had to flee Rome to Gaeta in Naples, to escape a rebellion by Italian Nationalists.

28th April, 1861

Is there not a dangerous lull, not only in the seething pot
of Napoleon's Europe, but in our own domestic condition?
There has been, for a few years past, a sort of liberalism of
profession and conduct in those who are of the high gentry
class, by which they have no doubt loathed the ill-feeling
which existed among the labourers and procured for them
many substantial advantages. But now we come to this stage
of things. These would-be liberals have no intention of giving
too much to the labouring population. They will procure
their own privileges, and their class feelings are, I suppose, as
strong as ever, but the labouring class, having got so far, will
not stop where they are, but will very naturally press on for
a more fixed recognition, and a wider grasp of power. Then
comes the revulsion: those who, to this point, have aided
them turn and oppose, and they, finding resistance where
they looked for aid, bring into the struggle all the acerbity
which springs from disappointed hopes, and embitter
every step by the charges of treachery, and the malice, so
proverbially born against 'unfriended' friends. And this
position promises to be more awkward, owing to the very
shaken condition of that anomalous party which has called
itself Whig, being in fact aristocracy making use of the
liberal weapons, and striking with them first on one side and
then on the other. When they are crushed out of the way the
two parties will, as of yore, be in force, and I fear experience
will show that with all the progress of the last generation,
there is still left that basis of human infirmity, which in every
age, has broken out somewhere, as if in protest against the
growth of peace in the world.

26th May, 1861

Long east winds, cold and cheerless, have given place now for 10 days to more genial weather: and nature, obedient to the touch, has sprung forward, like the bull when the door is opened, and he bursts on the arena with the first roar of his magnificent self confidence.

America, divided in itself, is drawing together its forces round Washington, with all the tokens of coming war. Jefferson Davis[1] has claimed the right to separate: the North proclaims their action to be rebellion. How far the real principle of liberty for the slave comes in can hardly be yet clearly stated. To all outward observation, in all public documents, pure and unadulterated motives of selfishness are put forward – showing it least, whatever may be the real views and thoughts of the statesman class, that they do not rank their fellow citizens above the predomination of this motive. A sad prospect for Western civilisation, still so closely bordering on much that is savage and unchristian, and so sure in a year or two of actual conflict: to sweep away the amenities of life, and to stand in the naked cruelty of backwood barbarism. Good Christians doubtless there are among them, active and energetic men, who will not spare themselves, but are these so numerous as to be of influencing weight on public action? And is the general public voice enough touched by the spirit of Christianity as to resist those overwhelming temptations to low and cruel issues, which grow as a matter of course out of a civil war.

---

[1] Jefferson Davis, President of the Confederate States at the beginning of the American Civil War.

Italy moves on its queenly course to Empire: feeling its way through many new and untried passages and showing a power of action and self-control which promises to lead her at last to established dominion.

Education has made a step here in the issue of the Education Commission Report,[I] on which men will brood for 8 months, and then their opinion will be given. It is, in small degree, a protest against the growing power of officialism, which, of all adhesive plasters, promises to cling the closest to poor old John Bull.

16th June, 1861

Cavour dead,[II] Napoleon alive and watchful, and all the rest of the world self-engrossed, except perhaps England, which sits watching the cats of France, which watches the mouse of Italy – the leopard of her arms couchant.

A week or ten days of bustle – Bishops Frome and Bridstow sermons at church openings, and then 'lest I should be exalted', break down tonight at Hentland on David the shepherd. Kati[III] and Mother here visiting and enlivening the solitude.

[I] The Royal Commission on the State of Popular Education in England, under the chairmanship of the Duke of Newcastle, was appointed in 1858 and published its report in 1861. It made recommendations regarding the education of the working class.

[II] Camillo Benso, Count of Cavour: Italian statesman and a leading figure in the movement towards Italian unification. The first prime minister of Italy; he died after only three months in office.

[III] His sister Katherine.

Lay[1] has a living (of Ingford) from the Bishop, and his gain gives me the trouble of looking for a curate. The change of them is incessant – Sheen, Kingsford, Burd, Lay – in 6 years or less.

21st June, 1861

Today comes the news of a debate on Wednesday 19th on church rates, when 274 voted on each side, and the Speaker, (Denison), gave his vote against the Abolition Bill, brought in by Sir J Trelawny. How many cases has the Speaker been called to vote in matters of real importance?

The question now is, what use is to be made of this victory – for the quieting and establishing of the Church. If church people say 'Oh, here's a great reaction, we may press our opportunity and fix our ideas firmer than ever', then is victory turned into defeat, and a fair opening for settlement thrown wantonly away.

The defence of a great cause is always maintained at disadvantage even against very infirm assailants. The fixity of position and the identity of argument which the unchanged position of the defender requires, become to the inconsiderate observer a cause of distaste, and even a feeling of repulsion. We know that this is altogether unreasonable: that an untried future naturally invites to hopeful anticipations, and allows of beautiful pictures of renovation, which

---

[1] Poole had a curate, Henry Lay, who at this time was living in his own house, ministering to Hentland, Hoarwithy and Little Dewchurch. Evidently he has received his promotion to an incumbency.

no experienced condition of humanity will permit us to entertain. The felicity of all classes which was to follow on Reform sweeping away, as we remember, all poverty from the land is but an image of the power which the very act of attacking puts in the assailants' hands. This is to say to draw a bright future – so impossible to deny its possibility, that already one half of the community is enlisted in the cause of any new thing. There is in so many minds a longing for change that the greatest recommendation which a proposal can have to them is that it brings about untried conditions of life. We are wearied with what we have known so long. This life, with all its constantly recurring events, is stale and flat; the dreary intercourse of daily life hardly disturbs its uniformity, and we feel that some startling attention will be like the breeze to the becalmed vessel. It will rouse our languishing minds to energy, will stir up those pulses within us which now for very tediousness are sinking into lethargy; and if there be some touch of danger, some rivalry of excited parties, why, this is of all things what we should most enjoy. As we cannot have a Revolution every morning with our breakfast, as the Americans will not oblige us by fighting a battle in time for every telegram, as even Italy rests a while to view its position after the death of its greatest statesman – then some change at home is the happiest alternative, and we welcome every stroke of party warfare which may shake us from the level of our calamitous monotony, which may obviate that greatest of life's evils, to lay down our paper after a careless glance, and say there is nothing in it today. And this feeling applies to Church Rules. It has been argued, re-argued, debated, presented in every possible form, in speeches and reviews, in magazines and leading articles. Divines have talked and written, and politicians have promised about it, even ministers have gone. It has become an old thing, and if it were [*stops here, as if he was interrupted*].

Church rates: in Poole's day, just as nowadays, it was a problem as to how to finance the Church of England. Up until that time, church rates for each parish were set by the churchwardens, together with the parishioners, at their annual meeting. The rate was a personal charge imposed on the occupier of a house or land in the parish, and it was compulsory. Failure to pay could mean a summons to the Ecclesiastical Court. However, this tax was often difficult to enforce, and especially so in the case of Nonconformists, who did not wish to support the Church of England when their own chapels depended entirely on their voluntary contributions.

As the nineteenth century wore on, popular feeling against Church Rates became more pronounced, and local Abolitionist Societies were formed, lobbying for the rates to be ended. There was much discussion in Parliament on the issue, but it was not until 1868 that the Compulsory Church Rate Abolition Act was passed, which made church rates no longer compulsory, but merely voluntary.

21st July, 1861

Among the rapid changes which are passing over the face of society, and bringing new notions into actual bearing on all sides, the mind turns with a feeling of relief to some mark of ancient life, some unbroken link between our fathers and ourselves. They become fewer every year. Traditional observances fall out of use. The 'cui bono'[1] injunction carries on its rigid search, and where 'idle old' admired, busy modernism sneers and sweeps away. Yet it is well that some

---

[1] 'who does it benefit?'

relics of ancient days should stand up amongst us in their pristine condition. It is a glimpse at old life, which gives us better understanding of the history, the struggles and the institutions which have floated on to us.

25th August, 1861

Temple[1] has a sermon in which he contrasts the inward and outward life of a man, setting forth that no one would recognise the identity of the two. The prominent features of one life being unnoticed in the other, and the fashioning points of the inward life not at all appearing in the record of the external movement. It is so in great measure with me: a life of intense immobility, with little of change, little of society, little intercourse with those who would lend a change to my thought-life.

1st September, 1861

Two of my friends, without any communication, and both of very good abilities for judging, have told me that a fault of mine is admiration of talents.

If it is so, it is a generous fault, for talent, abstracted from the use of it, like fire, or force, or wine, is as likely to do harm as good. But it is a force that moves the world, and therefore, certainly to be considered. I was not myself aware

---

[1]Frederick Temple: headmaster of Rugby School, Bishop of Exeter and later Archbishop of Canterbury.

of this propensity, and I had fancied that the direction in which talent was employed was not omitted in my balance of admiration. But it may well have been so, and I would endeavour to play off goodness against ability, and never to be led into admiration of that truly hateful sight, a man employing the gifts of God in utter disregard of the Giver. That I hardly think I do. But what I more probably have done is to despise and overpass the humdrum dullards, as they appear to me: people in all points perhaps my equals, and in many ways my superiors, and with a sort of latent enthymeme[I] to have lodged them far below my worthy self. Now, here is a real fault: I should remember Arnold: 'cap in hand', to such a one: and I should remember too that I am not Arnold, not in any way, or any point, for any reason justified in holding out the sign of superiority, to any plain-going Christian whatever; and though it may please and flatter me to hear and read the words of clever men, and so to seduce myself into a belief that I am one of the fraternity. Yet the safer and truer way is to hold out the hand of fellowship to 'whomsoever', esteeming others better than myself, 'sit scripturi factum'.[II]

To Garnstone[III] – Devereuxs, Clives, Scudamores, Freemans, Kings Hoptons.

To Foxley – 16 men in Garnstone garden, and neatness and excellence the consequence. Tecoma, Bidens, Geranium, Saponaria.

[I] A logical deduction, in which one of the premises is unstated.

[II] 'let it be written'.

[III] Garnstone Castle, Weobley, the home of Daniel Peploe, deputy lieutenant of Herefordshire. Those were the days when you could employ 16 gardeners!

8th September, 1861

The growing shades of the autumn evenings have now, at last, brought my third service to an end – a service less successful than some of the earlier years. The series of sermons was a poor one and needed much more care and study than I gave it, and for lack of this the life of David proved, I fear, but little interesting or profitable to my hearers. And now what shall I do with the hours to be gained from the evenings? Study or teaching? Shall I have some subject and diligently study it if I am allowed any evenings at all, or shall I invite my old scholars and some others to come and spend them with me. That perhaps will be the best, all things considered. My solitary ways need to be interrupted – my dilatory habits, my poverty of thought, all need the presence of others to rouse and keep me to the point. Then what to do with them? – so far to amuse them as not to desecrate the day. Let me look for some study that will answer for them.

15th September, 1861

The week of my stewardship of the Hereford Music Meeting,[1] which has proved, I hope, successful and generally satisfactory. 4 days: oratorios, 3 concerts and a Ball. The early services were excellently attended: Arkwright, Sir W Curtis, Col Clifford, Hawkshaw and self were the Stewards who acted. Shilling tickets were issued for the first time, and though done at the last moment were successful. To me it was an especially social and agreeable meeting, affording me many pleasant acquaintances and many renewals of old intercourse.

---

[1] The forerunner of today's Three Choirs Festival.

13th October, 1861

Another birthday has now passed over my head, and I am 42.
Twenty-one years have passed since I reached the recognised
age of manhood. How have these years been passed? Three
years were spent between Oxford, foreign travel, and living
at home, preparing for Ordination. Four and a half at St
Weonards, half a year at Homend on my father's death: then
at Lugwardine five and a half, and here at Hentland seven
and a half. Of this, the greater portion has been spent in the
solitude of a country parsonage. 'The solitude', I would hope,
'that makes the spirit pure'. Several times I have been to the
north of England, during this interval, once to France and
once to Scotland. Once to Weymouth and Brighton, and
sundry other excursions, none exceeding a month or 6 weeks
in duration. The relaxation I have taken has been chiefly in
the way of visits to friends' houses.

Surely this quiet and even life demands much thankfulness.
It is true that the restless spirit may at times wish for variety
and excitement, may pine for the consolations of society,
and believe that in the turmoils of busier societies, greater
usefulness might be reached, greater discipline exercised over
the secret world of thoughts. But these lives have their own
dangers, and when I think upon the especial weaknesses
and temptations to which I am most subject, I can easily
see that in civilised town life, or in the attractions of a more
intelligent and less boorish set to teach, to guide, to inoculate,
I might have not only failed to do them my bounden measure
of service, but even myself fallen into some hideous depths
of folly and sin, and gone mourning all my days in sorrow to
the grave. That this has not been so, I thank thee, O Lord,

from my heart, and I pray that thou of thy goodness will so confirm and strengthen in me all good things, that I may cheerfully accomplish what thou by thy providence showest me that thou wouldest for me to do.

One thing I may honestly say, that in all that I have done, and abstained from doing, as to the place of my clerical life and all the more important changes of my life, I have endeavoured to see what God would have me do. I have tried to see what by the complications of events, the actions of others, the 'accidents', as they are called, of life; the opportunities of action, the warnings not to act that He has been pointing out for my guidance. I may have been mistaken – perhaps in many things I have – but I do not believe that I have taken any step without a clear conviction that it was brought before me by His will. May I be enabled to continue this course, with a clearer insight into his dealings and a more thorough cheerfulness of acquiescence when the result contradicts my preformed wishes. O Lord, deal with me in thy wisdom, and if in any thing I desire what is not in thy sight good for me, strengthen me to a ready submission and hearty activity in other ways, to do my duty in that state of life to which thou shalt be pleased to call me.

27th October, 1861

De Tocqueville[1] says in one of his letters that the next convulsion that lies before England will not be political but

---

[1] French sociologist and political theorist Alexis de Tocqueville (1805–59) travelled to the United States in 1831 to study its prisons, and returned with a wealth of broader observations that he codified in *Democracy in America* (1835), one of the most influential books of the nineteenth century.

religious. And when we look at the extreme quietness, almost indifference, with which the catchwords of party, the best questions of politics are just now regarded, we can conceive that he may be right. No doubt some combination of circumstances may at any moment call out the party spirit of England, set class against class, and renew all the vehemence of '32,[I] or '45,[II] and then church matters would again sink into less prominent place. But if this should not occur, if we should glide on in our present course, it will be with an accelerating importance given to matters which concern the Church. And even now, the only questions which really raise keen discussion are ecclesiastical or doctrinal disputes: the intense bitterness which was shown in the cases of St Barnabas and St George's-in-the-East,[III] fostered and sadly strengthened by the good-natured laissez-faire of Sir G Lewis, gives a slight hint of what might be awoke.

I suppose high church people have in some measure profited by the history of Archbishop Laud,[IV] and we shall not see

---

[I] The British Reform Act of 1832 granted seats in the House of Commons to large cities that had sprung up during the Industrial Revolution, and removed seats from the 'rotten boroughs': those with very small electorates and usually dominated by a wealthy patron.

[II] 1845 saw the beginning of the Great Famine in Ireland, caused by potato blight, during which well over a million people died and two million emigrated. Prime Minister Robert Peel attempted but failed to persuade his Cabinet to provide famine relief and to repeal the Corn Laws which kept the price of bread artificially high.

[III] Another example of the tensions arising at this time between high-church and low-church sympathisers. For more details, see: https://en.wikipedia.org/wiki/St_George_in_the_East

[IV] William Laud, Archbishop of Canterbury 1633–45. Strong proponent of rule of the Church by a hierarchy of bishops, uniformity of practice in all churches of the C of E, and high church, ritualistic liturgical practices. Instituted placing altars in the sanctuary, surrounded by rails. Persecuted anybody with ideas different from his own. Eventually beheaded in 1645.

people driven into rebellion and uproar for a surplice or a
bow, but points of principle lie so close to foolish fancies,
and clergymen are occasionally so blind to what is going
on around them, that a few obstinate individuals may very
unexpectedly hasten an outbreak. Again, the utter failure
of the Anti-state-church League will embitter its leaders,
and give a fresh impulse to men whose life is passed in
a sort of atmosphere of agitation. It is life to them to be
organising, haranguing, petitioning, and while the clergyman
is unwillingly turned aside from his parish plans, his school,
his books, his society, his comforts, his private mode of life,
to act for a time the strange part of agitation, his opponents
are gathering fresh strength from their very labour. In such a
contest, must not the Church be outworked?

It is true that the strong and healthy portion of the upper and
middle classes is in very great majority on the Church's side.
But this gives the contest the disagreeable aspect of a class
question. And in many districts, it is as much a desire to be
apart from the richer ranks, which leads men to little meeting
houses, as from any doctrinal differences, or theological
purism. But there are still in the Church cases enough of
negligence and inadaptability. The clergy are still often enough
to blame, and the system of the Church has still blots enough
in its face to make the contest one not without danger. The
character of our confidence still remains, and with a good
cause if rightly manned, we may still be triumphant, and when
we think of all the good and holy capabilities which will die
with the Church of England, when we recall, how through
a period of almost infidel neglect, she has still reclaimed her
place, if not in the affection of all the people, yet in the respect
of all and in the love of many. We may work on under God's

blessing with cheerfulness and hope; no other existing church can supply her place. The freedom and order, the scriptural basis, and the traditional symbol: the growth of today, and the unbroken links of the past – all these place her alone in the Earth. But if so, her clergy should be alone among the clergies of Earth in their labour and self-denial, their high views and spiritual advancement. And though in respectability we may probably challenge every church that is, or ever has been, yet if we come to the meeting of principle, to the clash of mind against mind, it will need much more than decent conduct and orderly attention to bring men to acquiesce in our claims and to vindicate to the English Church its position in this land, bursting with energy and life.

1) Clergy need to be trained to controversy.
2) Need some more familiar links to tie them to the people.

23rd December, 1861

The English Church is pronounced in newspapers, on platforms, in Parliament to be strong in the affections of the people, to be steadily and rapidly gaining ground. Statistics are brought forward to prove this: the schools, the churches, the new Bishoprics, the revised interest in religious matters – all that has been done and is doing everywhere is pointed to as a triumphant confirmation of it. And as far as these things go, their tale is indeed true. Much has been effected, much is in course of construction, and yet the great question may be still unanswered whether the Church is doing its appointed work, and making its place safe against the hour of struggle. The Church of England claims a very peculiar place in the providential scheme of the World. She claims to be the only heir of that original church which the Apostles themselves founded, the only church now in the world (except those which have issued from her, and are combined with her) which presents to its children the full Message, in the full form which was delivered to the Christians of Alexandria, or Lyons, or Carthage. She does not maintain that she is in practice or rule at all identical with those early societies: there are wide divergences, and even contrarieties between them. There are things of which they have retained the names and lost the substance – there are points of very high importance valued in them of which she has lost the trace. She does not maintain, either, that there have not been and are not other churches which have received and held the substantial graces of the Faith which have through many ages conveyed and do still convey to their faithful children the gifts of God's Spirit sufficient for their Salvation. She does not proclaim that there are not in other churches points which she would do well to imitate, practices which are a lesson to her. But her claim is this – that in the two main branches of a church – the purity of Faith and the orthodoxy of practice – she stands alone.

31st December, 1861

I write the date of this year for the last time; and the year closes with a humbling incident, which I pray I may use to its appointed purpose. My evening service for the old year's death is rivalled by a meeting at the Chapel,[1] and a 'famous

---

[1] The chapel stands at the foot of the steep steps up to the church. Now a private dwelling, its Nonconformist roots must have been a thorn in William's flesh.

preacher' from Hereford made a sensible diminution of my congregation – a wholesome mortification. If I have taught here for 7 years, and not given any sounder basis, is there not something wrong? Have I not neglected something to conciliate the affections of the people, or to instruct them in the truth? There may be extenuating circumstances, or truly seen. They may aggravate my fault. Let me more carefully, tenderly and individually deal with people: watch them more closely, and converse with them more individually in unhasting diligence. O Lord, grant it to me. If Little Dewchurch is to be separated, and I live to see it, may it be the beginning of a new system to me.

[Prayer, ending with]
O Lord, bless these thy people committed to my charge: bless my mother and sisters, my friends and relations, and all who need my prayer. O Lord, hear me for Jesus Christ's sake, Amen.

5th January, 1862

The opening days of a New Year demand a grateful record: the soft, spring-like days, moistened with an actual April shower, with soft rainbow, and a clear young moon: the tokens of much diminished suffering among the poor, those too-abundant dwellers in so rich a land. Then the sounds of war have somewhat lulled; America seems to withdraw from the folly of ostentatious presumption, which she puts on so readily, and in the face of the grave, quiet earnestness of English preparation, reason has sprung up and obtained a hearing.

19th January, 1862

The Roman Catholics have their confreres, in which they
bind together with a feeling of brotherhood those whom
they would fashion to a common mode of action; and there
are many cases in which it would be most useful among
us: parochial brotherhoods of young men and sisterhoods
of young women, to meet at certain times, with certain
purposes, with a specified organisation and under due
direction. We have not, indeed, the 'Rosaries of Marie' or the
confreres of the 'Saint Sacrement': but there are other catches
to which they might respond tunefully. To recommend this,
and to apply to our county people the duties more especially
needed – to point out the dangers and peculiarities of their
position, it might be well to issue a series of Herefordshire
Tracts. Could we get people to work them plain – not clumsy,
but forcible, clear, argumentative, quite taking their level?
There are a few subjects which would seem to belong to them
especially:

1) the dangers of isolated dwellings, scanty population,
   uneducated youth, behind the age.
2) the peculiar form of dissent and indifferentism: 'I go
   wherever I get food'.
3) cider.
4) 'pot house clubs'
5) unneighbourly conduct.
6) want of independence
7) Church and Communion for gain sake.
8) want of bold, honest conduct,
9) grudging others.

2nd March, 1862

We are drawing on once more to Lent. Let me set myself some task, some duty, which may bring me to profit by the season: a definition of duty which is, rightly used, of real value. This again requires guarding, that it should be neither an idle form nor a snare. Therefore it is better to under, rather than overstate the intentions, and yet if this shrinks back into nothing, mischief again is so done.

Let there be then
1. An earlier rising.
2. An abbreviation of miscellaneous reading, in favour of books of practical improvement.
3. Study of the Bible.
4. Some definite parish work.
5. Some acts of self-denial and charity.

O Lord, enable me for Jesus Christ's sake to carry this out to the profit of my soul and the good of these thy people. Amen.

11th May, 1862

Lent has passed and gone, and Easter has again swept by us, and here I still find myself employing the last moments of the Sunday evening with these casual records. The school, so long talked of, is now in course of building, and is to be finished by September, and the completion of it will involve many changes in the parish, as the separation of Little Dewchurch will probably take place about the same time; I may then see the parish put into some regular working order.

Here the diary ends.

26th December. 1858.

Christmas is come & gone — Wet: and gloomy as ever dulled the more genial feelings which belong to it; by Prescription.

A more gradual amendment than I had hoped, has made this Week also useless for any parish Work—. and I still feel enough of the Remnants of Illness about me, & make me feel very uncertain as to the Future.

The Christmas Communion few both from the Wet, and from my long Inability to do as I had hoped in arguing with the

Afterword

WILLIAM BECAME A prebendary of Hereford Cathedral in
1867. In 1870, on the death of his mother, he inherited
the family home at Stretton Grandison, and huge estates as well,
which gave him the resources to take forward some of his projects:
to him Hentland and Hoarwithy owe not only the beautification of
both churches, but the building of the old school at Kynaston, the
reading room in Hoarwithy, (now Church House), the Vicarage
(now a private house) and the restoration of some of the cottages.
He was a Justice of the Peace for Herefordshire, and continued his
interest in education.

He continued his ministry in Hentland and Hoarwithy till
his retirement in 1901 at the age of 82. He died the following year.
Probate was granted on his estate for the sum of £76,917, the
equivalent in excess of £10 million in today's money.

If you have the chance to visit Hentland and Hoarwithy churches,
look out for some of their remarkable features, which are described
in the leaflets available at the churches. (There is also a good website
at: www.hentlandandhoarwithy.co.uk/hentland.html).

Hentland has its ancient preaching cross in the churchyard
with a faded image of Dubricius on the head. Its remarkable
decorated organ and wall paintings in the chancel from the
nineteenth century have undergone extensive conservation
recently. Below the church on the north-east boundary of the

Hentland School

Hoarwithy Church as it is now

churchyard is the spring and holy well which may have drawn people to this special site in the first place.

Hoarwithy Church has its beautiful loggia, much beloved by wedding couples for their photographs – the outdoor gallery with arched outer wall running along the south side of the church. Inside, the mosaic of 'Christ in Glory' over the altar grabs the attention, but don't miss the oak carvings in the chancel depicting the ancient British local saints Weonard, David, Cynog and Tysilio, all of them active Christian missionaries in these parts in the fifth and sixth centuries. On the panels on the ends of the choir stalls are carved scenes from the legendary life of St Dubricius, demonstrating Poole's interest in his predecessor's story.

Last but not least – as you stand on the chancel step, turn around and crane your neck to the west end of the church. High up in the apex of the roof is the little 'Angel of Doom' window, by Edward Burne-Jones and William Morris, in all its rich, glorious colours.

∾

REVD DR FRANCES PHILLIPS MBChB DA, FdA (ministry), is a retired associate minister of the St Weonards Benefice, which includes the parish of Hentland and Hoarwithy